DISCARD

DATE DUE

DISCARD

BRODART, CO.   Cat. No. 23-221

UNRESTRAINED

UNRESTRAINED

JUDICIAL EXCESS AND THE MIND OF THE AMERICAN LAWYER

ROBERT F. NAGEL

TRANSACTION PUBLISHERS
NEW BRUNSWICK (U.S.A.) AND LONDON (U.K.)

Library of Congress Catalog Number: 2008006952
ISBN: 978-1-4128-0743-2
Printed in the United States of America

Library of Congress Cataloging-in-Publication Data

Nagel, Robert F.
   Unrestrained : judicial excess and the mind of the American lawyer /
Robert F. Nagel.
       p. cm.
   Includes bibliographical references and index.
   ISBN 978-1-4128-0743-2
   1. Judicial power—United States. 2. Political questions and judicial
power—United States. 3. Justice, Administration of—United States.
I. Title.

KF5130.N345 2008
347.73'12—dc22   2008006952

To my brothers, Jack and Bill

Contents

Acknowledgments

The idea for this book began when I wrote a couple of magazine articles prompted by the nominations of Samuel Alito and John Roberts to the Supreme Court. Or, more precisely, I should say that the idea began because of correspondence received in response to those articles. This correspondence suggested to me that the way people understand the confirmation process may be changing. One part of this shift involves a growing appreciation for how difficult it is to change the behavior of the Supreme Court. For conservatives, of course, this appreciation is linked to intense frustration over decisions on issues like the separation of church and state, gay rights, and abortion. For liberals it is linked to anger over the Court's decision intervening in the 2000 presidential election in Florida and several decisions limiting the power of the federal government. Both sides seize on cases that mandate results that they dislike and couch their objections in terms of "judicial activism." But beneath the ideological differences there is, I think, an increasing understanding about how implacable the Court is in its commitment to the aggressive use of power.

A closely related development is the beginnings of a move from a narrow focus on the wisdom of the particular policies mandated by judicial decisions toward wider attention to the consequences of the Court's role for society as a whole. This change in perspective is assisted by a new recognition among some Democratic party activists of the political costs of making support for abortion rights a litmus test for elevation to the federal bench and, among interested people generally, of the cultural costs of making abortion policy a matter for the national government.

Since these shifting understandings resonate with themes developed over many years in my academic and journalistic writings, my correspondents (in short) made me think that now might be a good time to bring those ideas together and to sharpen and expand them. The legal, institutional, and cultural issues related to the Court's behavior are important not only to lawyers and academics but also to citizens more generally.

Therefore, while a substantial part of this book will, I hope, be of interest to fellow members of the legal profession, I have tried to write in terms that will be understandable and interesting outside the world of law and legal scholarship. To the extent that this has meant that I have taken the time to explain some matters already widely understood in the legal academy, I ask for patience among my professional colleagues.

I want to express my gratitude not only to those correspondents who urged me to write a book of this kind, but also to my research assistants Albana Alla and Kimberly Diego, who were especially helpful in sifting through the transcripts of confirmation hearings, and also Matt Weeber, who did copious amounts of research on the subject matter of Chapter 9. Pru Nagel read and commented on the whole manuscript. Paul Campos, Rick Collins, and Chris Mueller provided critiques of early versions of selected chapters. I am also grateful for the opportunity to present some of the material before academic audiences. Part of Chapter 2 and much of Chapter 3 was presented at a conference, sponsored by the Australian Research Council and held in Melbourne, Australia, on protecting human rights in Australia. Early versions of Chapter 5 were presented to faculty colloquia at Wake Forest Law School and the University of San Diego Law School. A version of Chapter 8 was delivered as the 2003 Brainerd Currie Memorial Lecture at Duke University School of Law. In addition, I received helpful comments from faculty colloquia at the University of Minnesota Law School and the University of Colorado Law School.

Inasmuch as segments of this book contain adapted versions of sections from my previously published writings, I also want to register my thanks for permission to use copyrighted material. Parts of Chapter 1 are adapted from "Advice, Consent, and Influence," 84 *Northwestern University Law Review* 858 (1990) and is used by special permission of Northwestern University School of Law, *Northwestern University Law Review* ; and from "Selective Justice," *Claremont Review of Books* 58 (2005); and from "The Problem with the Court," *National Review* 43 (Nov. 21, 2005), copyright 2005 by National Review, Inc., 215 Lexington Avenue, New York, NY 10016, reprinted by permission; and from Book Review, *Washington Monthly* 54 (May, 1996). Parts of Chapter 2 are adapted from "Judicial Power," *The Oxford International Encyclopedia of Legal History* (2008) and is used by permission of Oxford University Press; and parts of Chapters 2 and 3 are adapted from "American Judicial Review in Perspective," Campbell, et al., eds., *Protecting Rights Without a Bill of Rights: Institutional Performance and Reform in Australia* 225

(Ashgate, 2006). Other parts of Chapter 3 are adapted from "From *U.S. v. Nixon* to *Bush v. Gore*," *Weekly Standard* 20 (Dec. 25, 2000) and from "Our Destructive Drive for Political Revenge," *Wall Street Journal* A18 (Oct. 16, 1996), reprinted with permission of the *Wall Street Journal* copyright 1996 Dow Jones & Company, all rights reserved. Much of Chapter 5 is adapted from "*Marbury v. Madison* and Modern Judicial Review," 38 *Wake Forest Law Review* 613 (2003). Much of Chapter 6 is adapted from "Principle, Prudence, and Judicial Power," revised by permission from *The Judiciary and American Democracy: Alexander Bickel, the Countermajoritarian Difficulty, and Contemporary Constitutional Theory* edited by Kenneth D. Ward and Cecilia R. Castillo, the State University of New York Press, copyright 2005 State University of New York, all rights reserved. Much of Chapter 7 is adapted from "Bowing to Precedent," *Weekly Standard* 24 (April 17, 2006). Most of Chapter 8 is adapted from "Diversity and the Practice of Interest Assessment" 53 *Duke Law Journal* 1515 (2004). And parts of Chapter 9 are adapted from "Journalists and Judges," *Weekly Standard* 14 (Dec. 4, 2006); "Law Schools are Bad for Democracy," *Wall Street Journal* A16 (Nov. 2, 2004), and "Supreme Chaos," *Wall Street Journal* A18 (March 7, 2005), both reprinted with permission of the *Wall Street Journal* copyrights 2004 and 2005, Dow Jones & Company, all rights reserved.

1

A Ship that Will Not Turn

I entered law school in 1969, the year that Warren Burger replaced Earl Warren as the Chief Justice of the United States Supreme Court. In the world of law students and teachers there hung in the air a portentous sense that a dramatic and inspiring era of Court-imposed social change was about to end. President Nixon, after all, had campaigned against the Warren Court's revolutionary decisions expanding the rights of criminal defendants. Burger, Nixon's first nominee to the Court, told the Senate Judiciary Committee that the Supreme Court had no power to use interpretation to amend the Constitution or to legislate. When asked whether the Constitution has "a fixed, definite meaning," Burger referred to Justice Black's famous view that the words of the Constitution are very plain and should be given that plain meaning. Only a year after Burger's confirmation, the Court refused to invalidate Maryland's rule capping welfare grants to large families, and I watched as a cursing Legal Aid attorney reacted to the news by kicking a wastebasket across the floor of his office. The possibility of using constitutional interpretation to achieve welfare reform appeared to have dried up. More generally, legal scholars and activists were soon bemoaning the unimaginative and anti-progressive trends that they saw taking shape in the Court's decisions.

By 1972 President Nixon had placed Justices Harry Blackmun and William Rehnquist on the high court. Since then, Republican presidents have successfully nominated eight more individuals for (as of this moment) a total of eleven justices, and all were nominated for the announced purpose of reducing the amount of legislating from the bench. Even President Clinton's two appointments, Stephen Breyer and Ruth Bader Ginsburg, were presented as moderates who would refrain from extreme forms of judicial adventurism. In short, for roughly thirty-five years Republican appointees have had numerical domination of the Supreme Court and,

1

more importantly, during that period the American people have witnessed a continuous record of assurances from presidents and judicial nominees that the Court should apply, not make, law.

It is now widely understood that this prolonged effort to restrain the Court has not worked. The opposition among Republicans to the nomination of Harriet Miers as a potential successor to the meandering Sandra Day O'Connor reflected what by then had grown from a series of disappointments to a profound sense of betrayal. The solution seized upon in influential right-wing circles is to demand nominees with fully developed legal philosophies and conservative records. On the left, many criticized the Court's "activism" in restricting the national government's regulatory authority over interstate commerce and its intervention in the 2000 presidential election. Some Democratic senators seek a solution in demanding judicial nominees who will honor precedent and respect other indices of judicial caution.

While it is commonly recognized that the Court has remained, in some sense, a highly "activist" institution, the exact nature of its record since 1969 is debated. One informed depiction is of a "third way" between the egalitarian utopianism of the Warren Court that is still revered by many Democrats and the cultural conservatism that is the aspiration of many Republicans. A related but more simple-minded depiction is that the Court's decisions represent a form of political moderation. The reality, I think, is more striking and more surprising than either of these depictions.

A Moderate Record?

The reality begins with the fact that neither the Burger Court nor the Rehnquist Court reversed even one of the Warren Court's revolutionary decisions establishing new individual rights. Not *Griswold v. Connecticut*, which began the constitutionalization of sexual freedom, not *New York Times v. Sullivan*, which turned the regulation of defamatory speech over to the courts, and not *Brandenburg v. Ohio*, which even in this age of terrorism continues to protect most advocacy of violence. And not *Miranda v. Arizona*. Chief Justice Rehnquist himself wrote an opinion emphatically reaffirming *Miranda*'s constitutionally dubious rule requiring that police inform criminal suspects about their right to remain silent before questioning them. In its first term the Roberts's Court passed up an opportunity to reverse *Tinker v. Des Moines Independent Community School District*, the case that injected federal courts into supervising school officials' decisions about the limits to student speech.

· The conservative instinct to respect precedent might be thought to explain this sustained refusal to reverse course, but it cannot explain why so many Warren Court rulings have been energetically expanded. It cannot explain, for example, the rather complete transformation by the Burger Court of a principle against legally-enforced school segregation into a demand that school districts achieve racial balance through extensive busing programs. Nor can it explain the Rehnquist Court's expansion of earlier, limited rulings on separation of church and state into an aggressive campaign to stop government endorsement of religion, including non-denominational prayers at school graduations, student-led prayers at football games, and public displays of the Ten Commandments.

Even this is only the tip of the iceberg. Since 1970 the Court has established new rights undreamed of during the Warren Court era. Everyone knows of a few egregious examples, such as *Roe v. Wade*, the abortion decision. But the record does not end there. The original abortion decision, which was itself roundly condemned by some important legal scholars as having no legal justification, has been stubbornly extended to grant the right to minors and to protect even the procedure referred to as partial-birth abortion.[1] Indeed, in voting to reaffirm *Roe*, three Republican appointees, O'Connor, Kennedy, and Souter, made the most extreme claims for judicial power ever articulated in American history. These claims are consistent with the justices' apparent conviction, which surfaces now and again in cases involving high political risk, that judicial intervention is necessary to protect the nation from chaos and dissolution. Thus, several of the same justices that President Nixon appointed to the bench rushed to short-circuit the impeachment process by demanding that he deliver the Watergate tapes to a federal district judge. Much later, in the notorious case of *Bush v. Gore*, the Court settled the 2000 presidential election, apparently out of fear that it would be too dangerous to resolve a disputed outcome in Florida through the political process.

Moreover, the Court's ambitious record is not confined to a limited set of highly visible issues. It extends to every corner of public life. It includes an extensive campaign to transform gender roles, as well as significant efforts to rewrite defamation laws in all fifty states, to protect pornography and nude dancing and offensive language and flag burning, to require free public education of the children of illegal aliens, and to

---

1.   In 2007 the Roberts Court upheld a federal statute restricting partial-birth abortions, but it meticulously distinguished this statute from the Nebraska statute that had been previously invalidated.

normalize homosexuality. In a mostly forgotten foray, the Court even adopted Charles Reich's theories about "the greening of America" to announce that public assistance is a property right and that sixth-grade schoolchildren must be given a hearing before being suspended. The result has been far-reaching changes to public administration and educational discipline. Finally, even the despair of welfare rights advocates proved to be premature, as the Burger Court protected the right of the poor to receive publicly funded non-emergency medical care, and the Rehnquist Court boldly used a previously moribund constitutional provision (the "privileges and immunities clause") to extend protections for welfare recipients.

I should not leave the impression that the Court has intervened only to achieve progressive or left-wing objectives. Its power has been exercised to restrain the power of Congress to regulate commerce and to limit federal jurisdiction over state governments. The Court has also moved to expand some protections for property rights. It has cast doubt on certain affirmative action programs. As we have already seen, it interpreted the right to equal voting rights in such a way as to facilitate one of George W. Bush's presidential elections. Given Republican influence over Supreme Court nominations for almost forty years, conservative results are perhaps less surprising than the sustained record of progressive outcomes. Moreover, despite the howls of protest that they raised in some quarters, most of the conservative forays have turned out to have limited practical significance. Nevertheless, they are part of the amazing modern record of judicial willingness to exercise power.

I will provide a fuller account of the modern judiciary's record in the next two chapters, but already it should be clear that it is an understatement to say that thirty-five years of appointing justices for the announced purpose of reining in the Court has produced a moderate role for the high court. To insist that something more surprising and drastic has been going on than is conveyed by the word "moderate" is not, however, to deny that the Burger and Rehnquist Courts declined some opportunities to expand judicial power. In 1973, for instance, the justices declined to undertake the reconstruction of the structure of public education funding, and more recently the Court declined to cut off political debate on the wisdom of physician-assisted suicide. Nor do I wish to deny that the post-Warren Court has imposed very important limitations on previous lines of decisions, most notably concerning school desegregation and the rights of criminal defendants.

I say that efforts to rein in the Court since 1970 have not produced a moderate form of judicial power because, despite such limitations and pull-backs, the Court has boldly asserted authority over an astonishing range of political and social issues, has frequently set aside the judgments of both state and federal officials, and has claimed for itself a central role in maintaining the American political system. Trailing along in the Court's wake, innumerable federal and state judges have also intervened aggressively, if at a lower level of visibility.

Partial Explanations

One possible explanation for this surprising state of affairs is what might be called the Nixon Explanation. This hard-nosed, even cynical, view is that all those presidential calls for judicial restraint and all the reassuring testimony at the confirmation hearings should not be taken at face value. President Richard Nixon, for one, was not averse to the active use of national power. Perhaps, despite having obtained office partly by appealing to southern resentment towards "activist judges," he nevertheless nominated future justices who shared his general philosophy of government. Nixon, after all, was the politician who initiated vigorous racial affirmative action programs; he may have intentionally nominated justices like Burger who would do the same in the school desegregation arena.[2] As for the more conservative President Reagan, perhaps his calls for judicial restraint are best understood as heart-felt expressions of frustration at liberal judging, but not as principled opposition to judicial efforts to achieve conservative objectives like limiting the regulatory power of the national government.

Cynical or not, there is some truth in the Nixon Explanation. As many have noted, the language of "activism" and "restraint" is often used—and is understood to be used—as a political code rather than a principled effort to identify an appropriate role for the judiciary. Moreover, along with the persistent rhetoric about the need for judicial modesty during the post-Warren era, there have also been strong pressures in favor of a potent role for the federal courts. Nevertheless, while the Nixon Explanation is partially accurate, it is not fully satisfactory. One reason, as I shall detail in Chapter 4, is the strength and persistence of certain themes in testimony at Supreme Court confirmation hearings. For almost four

2.   A decision from the first term of the Roberts Court sets certain limits to the voluntary use of race by school authorities in their pupil placement systems, but casts no doubt on previous cases authorizing district judges to require the use of race-conscious assignments in order to make up for past discrimination.

decades now, nominee after nominee has contrasted the roles of the political and the judicial branches. One after another they have denied that justices should legislate or that they should change the Constitution. Even acknowledging the choreographed nature of the hearings, it pushes cynicism very far to attribute no significance at all to these apparently serious assertions. When even a modicum of significance is attached to the nominees' assurances and when their testimony is then compared to the unrestrained—often ambitious, occasionally stridently self-aggrandizing—record of the Court, some further explanation seems necessary.

A common supplementary explanation might be termed the Souter Explanation because of the observation that, when he was nominated, David Souter had little public record involving important issues and that he has turned out to be one of the most liberal members of the Court. Under this view, which had much to do with opposition to the Miers nomination, it is assumed that predictions about judicial behavior can become more accurate if there is enough information about the nominees' values and philosophy. The problem, then, has been that not enough was known about all or most of the justices nominated and confirmed after 1969.

There is, of course, also some truth in the Souter Explanation, but it does not fully explain our inability to restrain the Court either. One reason is that, while some presidents have claimed not to ask potential nominees about their views on specific legal issues and nominees have generally avoided answering pointed questions from the Judiciary Committee during their confirmation hearings, all the nominees since 1969 have had extensive careers involving them in important public issues. In addition to serving as appellate judges, most had held important positions in the executive branch or as legislative staffers at the federal level. O'Connor had been a politician and judge in Arizona. Scalia, Kennedy, Ginsburg, and Breyer had been visible as academics. Even Souter had been the attorney general of New Hampshire, a justice of that state's Supreme Court, and a judge on the United States Court of Appeals for the First Circuit. These records of involvement in public affairs should have provided a useful basis for predicting behavior on the Supreme Court. Nevertheless, the fact is that over more than three decades the Court has turned out to be far more inclined to intervene in politics and culture than anyone could have predicted.

This leads to the Kennedy Explanation, which posits that nominees' beliefs change radically once they are on the Court. Some of this shift is thought to occur simply because the position of Supreme Court justice offers such tempting opportunities to exercise power and such copious sources of ego enhancement. Much of the pressure to change is thought to be social. The justices, it is said, live in Washington D.C. in close proximity to people who think the purpose of life is to exercise political power over others. They begin to read the *Washington Post* and they socialize with trendy law professors from places like Harvard. Or, as in the case of Justice Kennedy (who is especially fond of relying on foreign legal sources when interpreting the American Constitution), they attend international judicial conferences where the prevailing belief is that judges are the ultimate guardians of civilized values everywhere.

Again, this explanation is surely partly true. But it is not true that the worldly professionals who have been nominated to the Court were innocent of "beltway" cultural influences before becoming justices. Most had lived in the nation's capital for years and had held important positions there. In fact, six had had the heady experience of serving as a clerk to a Supreme Court justice as one of their first jobs. Moreover, as indicated above, all of the future justices, whether living in Arizona or Illinois or Washington, D.C., were powerful judges or ambitious executive branch officials or assertive academics or successful partners in law firms before ascending to the Court. You would think, then, that some of the intellectual and moral hubris that is supposed to have developed after confirmation would have already appeared before that and should have been detectable during the nomination and confirmation processes.

From the recognition that nominees to the Court are not new to political power, emerges a fourth explanation, the Stevens Explanation. Under this theory, the record of the Court reflects the elite social and professional class to which most of the nominees belong. And it would be surprising if their backgrounds did not affect the justices' thinking. (Indeed, virtually all the nominees whose confirmation hearings are surveyed in this book acknowledged as much.) It seems possible, for instance, that Justice Stevens's evident hostility to governmental involvement in religion reflects in part a mid-western, upper-middle class disdain for southern fundamentalism.

Here, however, it is necessary to distinguish sharply between two aspects of what is surprising in the modern Court's record. It is surprising, on the one hand, that the Court has been so willing to use judicial power. And it is surprising, on the other, that much—but not all—of the Court's adventurism has been directed at progressive objectives like gay rights, abortion, contraception, and equality for women. While it may be plausible to believe that certain progressive political and moral values tend to be embraced by at least specific subsets of the elite social class from which the justices tend to come, a particular policy preference does not necessarily translate into a belief that it is appropriate to use judicial power to achieve that preference. Certainly American history provides examples of Brahmans like Justice Oliver Wendell Holmes who favored a tightly constricted judicial role even when this role sacrificed their strongly preferred policies. Thus even if modern justices are surprisingly "progressive" because of their class identification, it remains to be explained why they so often think that it is appropriate to use their positions on the high court to impose those values. For reasons that I will soon try to make clear, this latter question is more important than trying to explain where the justices get their values.

At any rate, the final explanation for the modern Court's behavior conceives of the objectives pursued by the modern Court as reflecting mainstream, rather than elitist, values. This explanation, which is based on some impressive evidence, is potentially the most important theory because it purports not only to explain but also to help justify the Court's modern record. I will call it the Bork Explanation, in honor of Robert Bork, whose nomination to the Court was rejected by the Senate in 1987. This explanation emphasizes that the American people approve of much of what the Supreme Court has done. That is, they like the policies imposed and, as long as they like these policies, they do not object to the fact that it is the Court that is imposing them.

The rejection of Bork, who is described by proponents of this theory as radical in his constitutional philosophy and reactionary in his politics, is seen as evidence that the modern process of aggressive questioning during confirmation hearings—far from being ineffective—actually has helped to ensure that successful nominees are usually somewhere in this mainstream. Bork, recall, was replaced by Anthony Kennedy, whom devotees of the Bork Explanation depict as a moderate. (The accuracy of this label is thought to be demonstrated by the fact that Kennedy eventually voted to reaffirm the basics of *Roe v. Wade*, the abortion decision that itself was originally thought to be radical both as a political and institutional matter.) If this were not enough support, they cite considerable evidence that over the years the Court's decisions have not strayed far from the political preferences of national majorities as measured by congressional behavior and opinion polls. In short, the Bork Explanation holds that the Court has been somewhat progressive because the American public is somewhat progressive, and as long as the Court pursues these somewhat progressive objectives the public does not object to the fact that the judiciary is exercising significant power.

It is true that that the policy outcomes imposed by the Supreme Court often track mainstream preferences and that Americans have been generally accepting of much of what the Court has done even when they do not approve of its decisions. But the Bork Explanation does not satisfactorily explain or justify the Court's record in recent decades.

To begin with, the precise mechanisms through which majoritarian values influence the justices are, to say the least, uncertain. One possibility is that the views that dominate during the confirmation hearings are accepted by the anxious nominees and also by sitting justices who are reading about the hearings (probably as reported in the *Washington Post*). This is certainly plausible as a partial explanation, but it sits uncomfortably with the fact that virtually every nominee to the Court has expressed the view, surely also held by many Americans, that a justice's task is to enforce the Constitution regardless of political pressures. Unless we indulge the unlikely assumption that these nominees also believed that the meaning of that document miraculously tracks present-day political preferences as expressed in confirmation hearings, the Bork Explanation requires us to believe that the justices' decisions can be explained on the basis of considerations that they emphatically assert should not influence them. Indeed, they would have to be implementing political messages conveyed in the very political events during which the nominees (and many of the senators) strongly assert the need for judicial independence from politics. As we shall see in Chapter 7, stranger things have happened. But to explain the Court's record over many decades on this basis would be odd (and insulting) enough to warrant looking for some additional mechanism through which majoritarian preferences are registered on the justices.

It is possible that the confirmation process, as well as other sources of political influence, explain Supreme Court decisions indirectly, in the sense that these influences tend to screen out anyone who does not have an approach to constitutional interpretation that is likely to produce results that are attractive to the majority of Americans. Thus, justices might be honestly utilizing interpretive methods, rather than reacting to specific political messages about desirable outcomes, but their methods might just tend to produce politically popular results. It is not impossible, but not very likely either, that senators are able—on the basis of a nominee's announced interpretive methods—to assure specific decisional outcomes that reflect the will of the majority. At least, senators in the modern era certainly work from that assumption. They ask, for example, about a nominee's respect for precedent on the theory that commitment to precedent will make a vote to overrule *Roe* unlikely. Similarly, the oft-repeated questions about whether the Constitution should be interpreted in light of modern conditions might tend to screen out nominees who will not vote for mainstream outcomes. Without question, politicians and observers often assume that an ardent commitment to implementing the framers' intentions will tend to produce morally constricted policy outcomes. That is a main reason that Robert Bork's originalism was such a cause of concern.

As widespread and reflexive as such assumptions are, they have an implausible side. Overruling precedent, after all, can and has led to some progressive and popular outcomes, such as the desegregation of public schools. A belief in interpreting the Constitution in light of modern conditions would seem to be a poor proxy for either progressive or popular outcomes because it is possible to assign completely opposite significances to those conditions. (Indeed, that is one common source of ordinary disagreement in any political dispute. The breakdown of the traditional family, for instance, can be seen as a reason to authorize gay marriage or as a reason to oppose it.) And it is surely peculiar to conceive of the constitutional framers as geniuses who designed the greatest form of government known to mankind (as most politicians, not to mention most Americans, do) at the same time that we posit that implementing their intentions will normally lead to results that most people would regard as undesirable.

In any event, whether confirmation hearings are thought to influence judicial outcomes directly or indirectly, it is unlikely that the confirmation process would produce majoritarian outcomes. Because each state has two senators no matter what its population, the Senate as a whole is not necessarily an accurate gauge of what the majority of Americans want. As an accurate institutional measure of the national majority's will, the presidency would seem to be at least as good as the Senate, and Robert Bork was President Reagan's choice to sit on the Court.

Nevertheless, some very prominent legal scholars, including Ronald Dworkin (about whom there will be more to say later), claim that even the work of the Senate Judiciary Committee can give voice to the views of "the nation as a whole." Specifically, Dworkin sees the Bork confirmation hearings as a rejection by "the country" of the "crude" theory that constitutional meaning should be based on the original intent behind the words. Instead, "the public" accepted a "jurisprudence ... of principle."

Now, these views must have been highly gratifying to Dworkin, as he has spent much of his professional life arguing for both of these positions. But the Judiciary Committee is even more unrepresentative than the full Senate, as it is selected largely by party leadership and dominated by highly unrepresentative members of a single profession, law. (Of the nineteen senators who made up the Committee when John Roberts and Samuel Alito were confirmed, fourteen were lawyers.) Is it at all likely that such a group could accurately represent a national consensus? Even Dworkin seems to recognize the implausibility of treating the Bork hearings as an expression of the people's will. Acknowledging that the proceedings did not amount to a referendum or a public opinion poll, he characterizes his claims as "an interpretive account." Keep in mind that for Dworkin an interpretation is not constrained by actual beliefs or intentions.

What can be seen in the Bork hearings, in fact, is not the expression of popular understandings but the gravitational pull of the legal culture. Senators were praised in the press for their learned questions on textualism, judicial restraint, the place of precedent in constitutional law, and other matters of legal philosophy. There were elaborate debates about arcane legal doctrines, including the proper standard of review in gender discrimination cases, subtle variations in the clear and present danger test, and the inter-relationship between fifth amendment due process and fourteenth amendment equal protection. Senators' brows were furrowed about whether the right to privacy can be found in a "penumbra" of any explicit right and about whether the category "political speech" is containable.

This fixation on legal philosophy and legal doctrine was natural for a committee made up of so many lawyers. Lawyers, after all, are more likely than other legislators to view legal materials uncritically. (They are, for example, less likely to see judicial interpretations as having been influenced by political considerations, and they are also less likely to attempt to limit judges' power.) Indeed, as the Bork hearings demonstrate, lawyer-legislators can be so entranced by the model of "the Judge" that they talk and act as if they themselves were jurists.

Worse, in attempting to carry on their jurisprudential discussions the lawyers on the committee were influenced, not by the American people, but by the legal establishment. Someone has to advise the senators on how to participate in judge-like conversations. Who better than the elites of the practicing bar and the academy? Is Bork outside the mainstream of legal thought? Better ask those who make up the mainstream. Hence not only the general values but even the specific pet theories of a few eminent law professors—theories about the unenumerated rights of the Ninth Amendment or the breadth of the principle involved in the contraceptive case, *Griswold v. Connecticut*—can momentarily masquerade as deep political consensus.

This professorial influence accounts for what seems in retrospect to be the dream-like quality of much of Bork's interrogation. Did senators really insist that constitutional text and framers' intent cannot serve as guides to interpretation and that a judge's fidelity to such materials would be inconsistent with a 200-year tradition? Did members of Congress actually welcome judicial readiness to negate legislative decisions and did they invite such actions on the basis of the justices' feelings about the "needs of the nation" or the fact of an individual's existence? And did politicians repeatedly take positions that could be characterized as supporting judicial solicitude for such politically controversial causes as homosexuality, obscenity, and subversive speech? All these lines of questioning did occur, and in the argumentative, intellectualized atmosphere of the hearings they did not seem to create political embarrassment for senators. But they did not exactly track the mainstream views of Americans. The questions certainly reflected ideas that were (and are) fashionable among legal scholars like Dworkin.

If neither the Senate nor its Judiciary Committee is especially representative, it could still be that majoritarian politics influence both the confirmation process and the justices in some diffuse way. Maybe by some form of cultural osmosis any group of educated people—maybe even the nine aging, unelected, atypical, insulated people who sit on the Supreme Court—can sense what most Americans will accept. At any rate, the proof of majoritarian influence would be that most major constitutional decisions are in line with popular opinion as measured by opinion polls. This explanation is less than satisfactory because it is essentially an admission that the specific mechanism that causes the justices to follow the people's wishes cannot be identified (unless they are basing their decisions on those polls). Moreover, the fact is that the Supreme Court has issued important rulings—for example, on partial-birth abortion, flag burning, term limits, and religious freedom—that do not coincide with the preferences expressed in polls. It is not enough to reply that the Court *usually* follows national majorities because some of the exceptional cases involve issues of extremely high emotional intensity and profound controversy. This at least throws doubt on any claim that the Court's record can be meaningfully explained as either a direct or indirect response to majoritarian pressures.

Even if it cannot be explained, many political scientists and legal scholars emphasize the degree to which Supreme Court decisions in fact do reflect majoritarian preferences and assert that this congruence constitutes a strong justification for the Court's performance. Few would contend, however, that majoritarianism is the only relevant value. Since there is no reason to think that the meaning of the Constitution always tracks popular political preferences, one obvious cost of political influence over the Court's decisions could be that some or even many of the resulting decisions are unfaithful to our fundamental law. An outcome that a majority of Americans like, or at least come to accept, may represent a radical or even a totally illegitimate use of judicial power. In fact, precisely that charge has been made by thoughtful jurists and scholars about *Roe v. Wade*, the very decision that proponents of the Bork Explanation claim represents mainstream thinking. At a minimum, it is clear that there is no reason to suppose that mainstream political outcomes will necessarily coincide with an accurate or appropriate understanding of the Constitution.

A political realist might reply that effectuating the popular will is more important than being faithful to constitutional meaning—even if politicians and judicial nominees are unwilling to say so. But the attractiveness of majoritarianism is not without limits even if we exclude constitutionalism as a consideration. Consider, again, the matter of intensity. Supposing that the Court is resolving explosive moral and political issues in ways that are acceptable to a bare majority of the people, the consequences to politics and culture may nevertheless be destructive, as I shall discuss more fully in Chapter 3. People may abandon the regular political process because it has become peripheral. Or they may enter that process with bitterness or anxiety because they believe the courts are resolving crucial issues in ways that ordinary voters cannot understand or hope to influence. Or they may become cynical about law and the judicial system. Politically accountable decision making processes have some important advantages that politically responsive outcomes simply cannot provide.

The intensity and centrality of the issues that the modern Court now routinely decides bear on majoritarianism in another way as well. To define a majority, it is necessary first to define the jurisdiction within which votes or preferences will be measured. The defenders of the modern Court assume that it is desirable for the Court to implement the preferences of a national majority. But especially when issues matter greatly to how people live their daily lives or understand their basic moral instincts or design their public institutions, it may be better to implement the majority will as expressed in the smaller jurisdictions of states or localities. On such issues, it may be important for people to know that public decisions will be made close to home by leaders who are familiar and accessible. It may be important to allow those for whom the outcome is insufferable an opportunity to find a different jurisdiction where a different outcome is possible. There is simply no doubt that, whatever mysterious force has impelled the Court to stay surprisingly close to the wishes of a national majority on many issues, the Court has frequently and emphatically reversed the decisions made by state legislatures and local school boards and city councils. Indeed, it has often reversed the decisions made by majorities in a majority of the states and sometimes, as in the abortion decision, the policies that had been adopted in all the states.

Finally, those who think that the Court's responsiveness to the will of national majorities is an explanation or a justification for its modern record pay too little attention to certain qualitative aspects of its opinions. In particular, the Court can announce and explain its decisions in ways that invite participation by political institutions in the interpretive process or it can preempt and condemn such participation. In recent years the Court has increasingly insisted on its own supremacy and has, correspondingly, condemned outside influences on constitutional interpretations. Quite independently of whether the justices guess correctly about what the public's preferences are, this growing authoritarianism has serious implications for the degree to which the Constitution is understood to be, on the one hand, an organic expression of popular will or, on the other, an imposed regime.

To summarize: Yes, it is true that promises about judicial restraint do not always signify a serious intention to reduce the role of the Court in American politics. And it is also true that the future votes of nominees to the Court are difficult to predict and that cultural influences seem to go to the heads of those elevated to the Court. And it is possible that the moral content of some judicial decisions can be traced to the social class from which many justices come. Finally, it is paradoxically also true that the Court's record seems to be partly a response to the justices' perceptions about what national majorities will find acceptable. However, if the Supreme Court's modern record is to be fully explained, and certainly if it is to be evaluated, we need to widen the inquiry.

A Fuller Explanation

Fortunately, a potent consideration is right under our noses. Indeed, the reason this consideration is usually ignored is because it is so obvious. It is this: those put on the Supreme Court are successful lawyers. This means that the justices are adept at—and therefore not inclined to be skeptical of—the way lawyers and judges think. Or, to use the more rarified language of the political scientist, Thomas Keck, the lawyers who make up the high court are affected by "inherited, institutionalized norms—such as particular conceptions of the Constitutional order and the judicial role." But where do those lawyerly norms come from? Why were these ways of thinking not significantly modified or abandoned after the end of the Warren Court? And how is it that professional norms, some of which emphatically call for prudence and restraint, operate to encourage boldness and, sometimes, arrogance? Much of this book is an effort to answer these questions. It is an exploration of why the way that American lawyers and judges think—whether they are liberal or conservative—is one of the basic reasons that we have such an insistently powerful judiciary.[3]

The way that modern lawyers and judges think is remarkably uniform and not really mysterious. The basic patterns, as I shall describe more fully in Chapter 4, are visible in the confirmation hearings of virtually every successful nominee to the Court since 1970. The elements of this jurisprudential consensus are: (1) Although as a realistic matter judges cannot entirely escape the personal and the political, they should endeavor to minimize such influences by attending carefully to traditional legal materials such as constitutional text, prior judicial decisions (or precedent), and political practices. (2) These traditional legal materials constrain judges by providing authoritative principles. These principles, in combination with certain legalistic aspects of the adjudicatory process, can create acceptable limits on the tendency for judges to impose their own preferences. And (3) to the extent that judging and lawmaking nevertheless overlap, jurists can still fulfill a distinctively legal function by exercising reasoned judgment.

As I shall explain in subsequent chapters, one significant part of the problem with this intellectual framework is that it provides no effective

---

3.   Other countries, particularly Israel, have powerful judiciaries, and a number of countries are moving toward the American model. It is not my purpose in this book to claim or imply that lawyers in all these countries think as American lawyers do. Obviously, there can be many different causes, specific to a country's history and culture, of what I am calling judicial excess. I do think that some part of the international movement toward American-style judicial power can be attributed to the example set by the American Supreme Court and to the influence of American legal thought.

constraint on judges' discretion to decide cases as they wish. Attention to multiple sources of legal authority, for example, begins with a free choice about which source to treat as determinative in any particular case. Moreover, the effort to escape the personal and the political by "reasoned judgment" badly misconceives the nature of moral decision making in the public arena and leads to self-delusion, not constraint.

An equally important problem, which is even less appreciated in legal circles, is that the main components of modern legal thinking interact in ways that impel judges to use their power aggressively. One of these components is the effort to combine realism about the nature of judging with a simultaneous commitment to traditional legal authority; another is the effort to qualify principled decision making with a commitment to self-discipline and restraint. For reasons that will be elaborated in Chapters 5 and 6, both of these combinations have psychological consequences that largely explain the imperialistic role of the modern Court. Similarly, as I explain in Chapter 7, the universal reliance on multiple sources of legal authority tends to break down into an over-riding devotion to precedent and to the institutional prestige of the Supreme Court.

The way that lawyers think about law and judging does not operate in a vacuum. The fact that the justices are successful lawyers means that their purposes, ambitions, instincts, and even personalities are formed by certain educational and professional experiences. These experiences, and their practical significance in magnifying the consequences of the dominant understanding of the nature of legal interpretation, will be examined in the final chapter.

Even if I can make this explanation convincing, there are strong reasons to ignore or resist it. Some will want to ignore it because they approve of many of the policies imposed by the Court or hope that some future Court might impose policies that they favor. But a major theme of this book is that pervasive reliance on judicial power to resolve important political and moral issues has destructive cultural consequences even if the specific outcomes of judicial decisions are desirable as a matter of policy or law. These consequences, which include political alienation and anxiety and conflict, should be of concern to people across the political spectrum—moderates, progressives, and conservatives. This is why I said that the important question about the modern Court's record is not why it pursues surprisingly progressive policies but why it is surprisingly willing to exercise power.

Others will resist the implications of my argument because it is difficult to see what can be done to rein in the Court if the cause of its behavior is something so basic and unalterable as the nature of law, legal training, and the legal profession. In this day and age, it is not realistic to think about putting non-lawyers on the Supreme Court. And even if this sacrilege were to occur, any justices without legal training—no matter how independent—would find it extremely difficult to operate effectively

Of course, changes in legal education could be proposed, and these might eventually alter the way in which law is thought about and practiced. The current emphasis in law schools on appellate cases and judicial decision making could possibly be reduced, courses could be changed to give due regard to empirical issues, and the overwhelming left-wing bias on law faculties might even be mitigated. But the fact is that law is a highly useful profession as it now is. In the ordinary carrying out of their tasks, lawyers contribute mightily to peaceful dispute resolution. They help people think carefully and methodically about how to solve both private and public problems. They have important roles in enforcing the law and in operating large organizations. And they play an inventive and energetic part in politics. Lawyers may be joked about, but they are often useful and sometimes noble. Many of the aspects of legal thinking that I am going to suggest are dangerous at the level of the Supreme Court (and in judging generally) are necessary elsewhere.

The situation, if forthrightly confronted, is discouraging but not entirely hopeless. If the root cause of judicial excess is the way lawyers think, it might help to change the way in which the records of judicial nominees are evaluated. Although I believe that even accurate predictions about specific positions that a nominee will take once on the Court will not change the basic direction of the Court, it might help to look for lawyers who are confident enough and independent enough to challenge established patterns of thought and deeply ingrained instincts. Such lawyers do exist. In fact, even some of the justices that have participated in creating the Court's modern record show encouraging, if limited, signs of skepticism about modern legal practices. Justice Stevens, for instance, has been doubtful about the appropriateness of elaborate constitutional doctrines that come to stand in the place of constitutional meaning. Justices O'Connor and Breyer have often resisted the allure of overly abstract thought. Justice Scalia has mounted a vigorous challenge to the widespread practice of defining American political traditions according to how the justices think those traditions should look. And Justice Thomas is far more willing than his colleagues to depart from prior decisions when those decisions can be shown to depart from the intended meaning of the Constitution.

But how to find lawyers who are capable of a more sustained and comprehensive independence from the professional norms and instincts that are causing the Court to play a destructive role in politics and culture? To do this, it would be necessary to look beyond a nominee's credentials and ideology. It would be necessary to attempt fewer predictions about voting patterns in future cases and to look more closely at general attitudes about the social costs of judicial intrusion into politics. It might be helpful to include more candidates who are less conventionally successful or have been successful by challenging established practices. Certainly, the strong tendency to select nominees from federal courts of appeal (eleven of the last thirteen nominees served in this capacity) should be stopped. In any event, to find justices who are capable of detached skepticism about entrenched practices, it would certainly help to end the domination that lawyers—and their assumptions and instincts—have in the membership of the Senate Judiciary Committee.

But even with this shift in assessment of potential justices, it is necessary to recognize that the nomination and confirmation processes will not by themselves be adequate to restrain the Court. Renewed attention needs to be directed at other political checks on the federal judiciary—checks such as limiting jurisdiction and reversing egregious errors through constitutional amendment and perhaps even imposing term limits. If the underlying problem lies with legal training and instincts, the solution must come from the larger community. The melodrama of confirmation hearings is less important than the political will to respond to judicial excesses.

It might be objected that political checks are unrealistic because in modern times Americans have proven themselves to be amenable to, even attracted to, a powerful judiciary. That is probably so. Nevertheless, there remains an unappreciated common interest in turning the Court from its course. Most political and scholarly attention is directed, in one form or another, at the issue of judicial activism, that is, whether the Court's decisions are unjustified as a matter of law or unwise as a matter of morality and policy. My hope is that this book will help direct attention away from misleading and largely fruitless arguments about activism. The important issue, I say again, is the degree of power that the Supreme Court and all those trailing lower courts are exercising. It is this—the centrality of the issues decided, the range of the issues removed from the political domain, the detail of the requirements imposed by the judicial rulings—that creates the cultural damage that is so often ignored.

The failure to recognize this damage is an intellectual problem that, I hope, can be addressed. If, as certainly seems likely, a fuller recognition of the nature of the problem that we all face does not budge the great historical and political forces that are in play, there is still value in fuller understanding. A more accurate appreciation of why the modern Court behaves as it does and what the consequences are—these are to be wished for even if little can be done to alter the Court's relentless course. At any rate, the first step is to describe more fully the nature of the modern exercise of judicial power.

2

The Rise of Judicial Power

As far back as the eighteenth and early nineteenth centuries astute observers, including Edmund Burke and Alexis de Tocqueville, noted that Americans tend to hold the legal process in high regard. Nevertheless, attitudes toward judicial power were cautious in the beginning. Under the Articles of Confederation the only national courts established by Congress were limited to adjudicating cases involving the seizure of ships. During debates over ratification of the new Constitution, broad agreement on the need for national courts was accompanied by considerable modesty about the nature and scope of their function. For instance, important proponents of the Constitution assured skeptics that the proposed federal courts would have no power to require states to submit to judicial authority as defendants in lawsuits. Moreover, some Anti-Federalists doubted that federal courts could be trusted to enforce constitutional limitations on national power or even to honor the natural meaning of constitutional text. Alexander Hamilton's famous defense in *The Federalist* No. 78 was that the judiciary would be the least dangerous branch of government because it would have so little influence over society and, indeed, would have no power to take any "active resolution whatever."

Some, including Hamilton, did think that the federal courts would have a useful role in preventing the other branches from violating the Constitution, but most assumed that the main protection against abuse would be popular resistance. This assumption grew naturally from the general belief that sovereignty resided, not in the courts (or any other governmental institution), but in the people. For those who had recently fought a war for independence and were in the process of debating and ratifying their fundamental charter, the political nature of sovereignty was an urgent and natural reality.

The new Constitution itself subjected the federal courts to important political checks. It vested the judicial power in one supreme court and such inferior courts as Congress might establish. Congress had authority to make exceptions to the jurisdiction of the Supreme Court and, within broad limits, to define the jurisdiction of the lower courts. Federal judges were to be appointed through nomination by the president and advice and consent by the senate. While they would enjoy life tenure and undiminished compensation, judges could be removed through the impeachment process. Federal criminal trials were to be by jury (an important venue for the expression of the popular will), and judges were specifically instructed that no one could be found guilty of treason except on the testimony of two witnesses to the same overt act. More generally, the new federal judicial system would operate alongside existing state systems. Thus federal courts, like other federal institutions, would be constrained by competition from state governments that would have the natural advantages of locality and familiarity. In fact, although a system of lower federal courts was created by the Judiciary Act of 1789, Congress did not give these courts general authority to hear cases arising under the Constitution or laws of the United States until 1875. For the first eighty-six years of the nation's history, judicial protection of federal statutory and constitutional rights was entrusted primarily to state courts.

Opposition to the proposed constitution produced assurances that, upon ratification, new rights would be added to the document, and the resulting Bill of Rights was largely directed at constraining federal judges. Search warrants were not to be issued except upon probable cause and with particular descriptions of what is to be searched. Indictments for "infamous crimes" were to issue from grand juries. No person could be tried twice for the same offense, nor be required "to be a witness against himself," nor be deprived of life, liberty or property without due process of law. Criminal trials were to be speedy and public, and defendants had the right to know the nature of the accusation, to confront hostile witnesses, to offer their own witnesses, and to have the assistance of counsel. The right to a jury trial was extended to civil damage cases. And, finally, judges were not to demand excessive bail, impose excessive fines, or require any cruel and unusual punishment. Plainly, Americans understood that the judicial process could be abused and intended that the work of federal judges be subordinated in significant ways to the will of the people.

From these cautious beginnings judicial power in the United States has gradually grown to the point where, as I have said, it is used to resolve fundamental moral and political issues, to initiate profound changes in society, to control public institutions, and, in significant ways, to supplant the sovereignty of the people. This remarkable development has been partly the result of initiatives by judges themselves, sometimes in the face of bitter popular disapproval. But it has also been a consequence of deep-seated American attitudes towards lawyers and law, attitudes that have often translated into political acquiescence to the growth of judicial power and sometimes into active encouragement.

Judicial Power in the Nineteenth Century

Modern use of judicial power is often traced back to *Marbury v. Madison* (1803). Oddly, however, this decision in many ways is reflective of the cautious attitudes toward the federal courts that had characterized the ratification period. In *Marbury* the Supreme Court held, in an opinion authored by Chief Justice John Marshall, that it did not have jurisdiction to order the secretary of state to deliver an official commission to a justice of the peace who had been appointed to his post by John Adams, the previous president, just before leaving office. The Court lacked jurisdiction because in its view the attempted grant of jurisdiction in the Judiciary Act of 1789 was inconsistent with the terms of Article III of the Constitution. The Court thus refused to enforce a federal statute that it believed to be unconstitutional despite the judgment presumably made by Congress that the statute was constitutional. However, even as the justices asserted this important prerogative, which is now referred to as the power of judicial review, it was declining the opportunity to order a high executive official to obey the law governing judicial appointments. In short, Marshall's opinion asserted a broad power to determine the constitutionality of federal statutes but did so under circumstances that avoided confrontation with the political branches and emphasized the judiciary's capacity for self-denying fidelity to constitutional limitations.

Despite a reference to the right of a sovereign people to establish their fundamental law, *Marbury* did not attempt to justify the power of judicial review with any evidence that the drafters or ratifiers of the Constitution intended that courts have the power to reject the judgments of the political branches about the meaning of that document. Instead the decision rests mainly on a series of inferences from the nature of written constitutions and the judicial function. While modern authorities differ significantly in their evaluations of the persuasiveness of the reasoning in *Marbury*, most agree that it is best understood as establishing only a limited power. For example, many argue that the power of judicial review only entitles a court to decline to enforce a federal statute in the case before it and, therefore, that the judicial interpretation of the Constitution does not bind other officials in the performance of their own duties. These duties might include, for example, (in the case of a president) deciding whether to veto a bill or (in the case of a member of Congress) whether to enact a new piece of legislation.

A second—and highly influential—understanding of the nature of the power of judicial review is that courts should override political judgments about the meaning of the Constitution only when that meaning is plain and the political branches have made a clear error. Under this view, constitutional interpretation is necessary not only to the application of law in adjudication but also to the processes of enacting and executing laws. Accordingly, all departments and levels of government have a responsibility to understand and protect the Constitution, and courts will normally defer to political efforts to exercise that responsibility.

The idea that the judiciary's role in enforcing constitutional norms is secondary to political enforcement was, with some exceptions, vindicated by actual practices during much of the nineteenth century. For roughly thirty years after *Marbury*, Marshall's Court itself gave considerable deference to both national and state legislatures. In 1849 the Court went so far as to hold that the provision guaranteeing each state a republican form of government involved "political questions" and therefore was to be enforced by Congress, not the judiciary. And after *Marbury* the Supreme Court did not invalidate another act of Congress until 1857, when in *Dred Scott v. Sanford* it declared the Missouri Compromise unconstitutional. This decision departed dramatically from the model of judicial power presented by *Marbury* in that it had major political consequences and put the Court in confrontation with both the Congress and the president. *Dred Scott* was widely criticized as legally unfounded and politically disastrous. Abraham Lincoln denied that the Court's interpretation of the Constitution should be binding on the president outside the confines of the particular case.

Four years later during the Civil War the Court held that Lincoln's suspension of the writ of *habeas corpus* was unconstitutional, as was the arrest and detention by the military of a citizen, John Merryman, who was not subject to the rules of war. President Lincoln publicly took the opposite position on his power to suspend the writ, and for some time his military, in defiance of the Court's order, refused to release Merryman. More importantly, the administration continued to subject civilians to military detention. Public criticism of executive defiance of the Court was slight. In 1866 the Court boldly ruled that the president could not authorize the trial of civilians, accused of insurrection, by military tribunals where regular courts were open and operating. It even announced that Congress had no authority to establish such tribunals although that issue was not before the Court. This decision, titled *Ex parte Milligan*, was a second important departure from the earlier practice of deferring to constitutional decision making by the political branches. However, as it was issued a year after the end of hostilities, the opinion had no effect on the conduct of the war. It did not even prevent widespread use of military courts in the South during Reconstruction. During this period the practical subordination of the Court to the political branches was also evidenced by congressional acts altering the number of justices sitting and limiting the Court's *habeas corpus* jurisdiction, a limitation that applied to a pending and highly significant case.

During the last twenty-five years of the nineteenth century, the Court began to use the power of judicial review more forcefully. The number of invalidations of federal statutes rose, and some of these decisions sharply limited congressional efforts at reconstructing the South. State legislative enactments were not immune from judicial oversight, as courts began to restrict state authority on the theory that the Fourteenth Amendment's due process clause protects certain substantive individual rights. In an effort to protect the free flow of commerce from the effects of strikes, federal courts also began issuing orders (called injunctions) that severely restricted union activities. In 1895 the Supreme Court approved these judicial intrusions into the traditionally executive domain of controlling civil unrest by ruling that the judiciary possessed inherent authority to punish union strikers who disobeyed injunctions. In that same year, relying again on its own understanding of the commerce clause of Article I, the Court significantly narrowed the reach of a federal anti-trust statute by distinguishing monopolies in manufacture from monopolies in commerce itself.

Although toward the end of the century the primacy of political enforcement of the Constitution was beginning to erode, by modern standards judicial power remained limited. For instance, in a series of decisions involving suits brought to enforce the rights of bondholders, the Supreme Court denied that lower federal courts had the power, even in the face of the complete intransigence of local officials, to appoint receivers to levy or collect taxes. During this period, lower federal courts did gain jurisdiction over federal statutory and constitutional claims. However, statutory schemes were less pervasive than Americans have become accustomed to in the modern era, and the Bill of Rights did not apply against state and local governments. The main protection for what are now thought of as federal Constitutional rights, including free speech and religious freedom, continued to rest, as it had earlier in the century and before, not with judicial review at either the federal or state level, but with state legislative enactments. The gradual abolition of official state churches during the early part of the nineteenth century, for example, was accomplished through such enactments.

Judicial Power in the Early Twentieth Century (1900-1937)

During the first four decades of the twentieth century reliance on judicial power grew, but the complex set of changes that would produce the modern role of the judiciary did not begin in earnest until about 1937. It is true that before 1937 courts continued to use the due process clause of the Fourteenth Amendment to invalidate a range of state laws. In *Lochner v. New York* (1905), for instance, the Supreme Court declared unconstitutional a state statute that prohibited bakers from working longer than ten hours in a day. In form, at least, the decision continued the long tradition of setting aside only laws that were clear constitutional errors. The justices conceded that states had wide authority to restrict the liberty of contract. The Constitution, said the Court, merely requires that the regulation serve some public purpose but the labor law in question served no such purpose at all. In dissent, Justice Oliver Wendell Holmes, making the kind of accusation that would become familiar in the second half of the century, charged that the Court was enforcing its own philosophy rather than the content of the Constitution. While cases like *Lochner* involved the judiciary in the legislative domain and thus presaged aspects of the modern era, their impact was limited because in a number of cases the Court, crediting the legislatures' objectives, allowed state regulation of economic activity. Moreover, by the mid-1930s the Court had begun the practice, which it has followed since, of generally deferring to legislative decisions regulating property rights.

The notion that judges could use adjudication systematically to achieve broad social consequences, however, did appear in at least two areas. First, in the 1920s federal courts used highly detailed injunctions to prevent organizing activities by labor unions. These amounted to regulatory codes and affected the economic welfare of workers across the nation. In 1932, however, Congress enacted legislation protecting important aspects of union organizing from judicial decrees. Second, during the Great Depression the Court invalidated significant components of the New Deal. Until 1935 the Court's interpretation of Congress's enumerated powers had allowed for considerable political discretion. But in that year the justices struck down the Railroad Retirement Act, and thereafter the Court voided important parts of the National Industrial Recovery Act, the Bituminous Coal Conservation Act, and the Agricultural Adjustment Act. If it had continued in this way, the Supreme Court might have prevented or fundamentally altered the modern administrative state. President Franklin D. Roosevelt, however, criticized the Court and proposed to "pack" it with new, younger members. Regard for the independence of the judiciary led to the failure of this proposal, but in 1937 the justices began to reverse course and soon approved the National Labor Relations Act and the Fair Labor Standards Act. The Court did not again impose any limitation on Congress's power to regulate commerce until 1976 and did not attempt another restrictive definition of interstate commerce until 1995.

Some of the most important judicial opinions of the early part of the century had to do with reconciling freedom of speech with national security. These decisions generally upheld convictions under the Espionage Act and state criminal anarchy statutes. Nevertheless, ideas about the purpose of the First Amendment and about the role of courts in society began to develop that would propel the courts during much of the modern era into an extensive campaign to protect speech from legislative and executive power. The central—and now familiar—idea, developed mainly by Justice Holmes in a series of dissents in cases involving exhortations to resist the war effort, was that speech should be protected until there is a clear and present danger of illegal action. That this idea could severely displace the authority of the political branches to gauge danger and to prevent harm can be seen in the implications that Holmes himself acknowledged in his dissent in *Gitlow v. New York* (1925). Gitlow had been accused of inciting the overthrow of the government by force or violence. Holmes argued that Gitlow's speech should be protected because it presented no immediate threat of overthrow. But what of the longer run? Holmes wrote, "If, in the long run, the beliefs expressed in proletarian dictatorship are destined to be accepted by the dominant forces of the community, the only meaning of free speech is that they should be given their chance and have their way."

If Holmes did not draw back from a far-reaching interpretation of the free speech clause, in *Whitney v. California* (1927) Justice Louis Brandeis envisioned a role for the courts dramatically greater than merely deciding cases. While in the case at hand Brandeis voted to punish subversive speech, his lyrical opinion painted a picture of courage and tolerance in American history. His glowing portrait and poetical language were an effort to protect speech by helping to consolidate a political mythology (and thereby to shape American culture) that honors the right to dissent as a central tenet.

By 1937, then, the American judiciary, led by the Supreme Court, was showing signs of a willingness to second-guess legislative judgments, to impose political outcomes in a systematic way, to adopt daring ideas, and to use judicial opinions for purposes far transcending the resolution of particular cases. These signs were not yet fully realized by any means. But in 1938 the Court offered in an unassuming footnote another sign, a suggestion about the direction the fuller use of judicial power might take in the decades to come. The case itself, *United States v. Carolene Products*, reaffirmed a version of the old rule that only laws that are clearly unconstitutional should be struck down by a court, but its famous footnote suggested that less deference should be given where prejudice prevents the political process from operating properly. Thus, as the modern era began, there quietly emerged the conception of judicial power as antidote to defects in the political process.

The Modern Era (1938-2008)

The complex set of developments that produced the modern characteristics of judicial power all had historical antecedents, some going back a decade or so prior to 1937 and some going back centuries. But these developments came together with great force after 1937. Given the significant and respected role that lawyers had long played in American government, it seems at first perplexing that the modern role of the judiciary did not fully emerge until after 1937. If, as the subtitle of this book insists, modern judicial excess is in important part attributable to the mind of the American lawyer, why did the components of the Court's distinctive modern role not come together until well into the twentieth century?

The answer to this question is that the mind of the modern American lawyer did not fully take shape until three developments had taken place. First, the case method (the significance of which I will discuss in Chapter 9) had to become an important method of legal education. This occurred at the end of the nineteenth century. Second, institutionalized legal education (as opposed to apprenticeship in a law office) had to become the predominant route to practicing law. This did not occur until early in the twentieth century. Third, a realistic understanding of law had to be combined with older, more formalistic understandings. This began early in American history but was accomplished in a systematic and self-conscious way between about 1920 and 1940. The consequences of these three developments will occupy much of the rest of this book. For the present it is enough to note that by the late 1930s important forces shaping the mind of the American lawyer were, like the legal events that I will now describe, combining in potent ways.

· The first of these events involved the idea that some or all of the Bill of Rights are protected by the due process clause of the Fourteenth Amendment and thus restrict state governments as well as the national government. The theory made a limited and tentative appearance as early as 1897, gained some traction in the 1920s and early 1930s, but only came to apply to nearly all of the listed rights between about 1940 and 1970. This doctrine of "incorporation" means that a wide range of state decisions have become subject to judicial oversight. This oversight could be achieved in practical terms because the Court had decided in 1908 that, while states are generally immune from suit in federal court, state officials do not share this immunity and are subject to injunctive orders. The Court extended the range of judicial oversight in 1961 when it broadly interpreted section 1983 of the Civil Rights Act of 1871, which allows for damage awards against any person who deprives someone of a constitutional right 'under color of law.' This ruling permits suits against local officials even when they act without legal authorization and vastly increased the number of suits brought to enforce constitutional rights. Then in 1978 the Court announced that a municipality is a person and thus is subject to damage remedies and injunctive relief for violating constitutional rights. By 1990 it had ruled that a district judge may impose bankrupting fines on a city as a means to force its council members to enact an ordinance thought necessary to correct housing segregation.

Other changes also augmented judicial power. Suits by multiple parties (now called "class actions") have a long history, but in amending the Rules of Civil Procedure in 1938, the Court for the first time formally recognized damage remedies in such suits and thus raised to prominence the device known as class suits. The possibility of obtaining monetary awards for many thousands of people gradually generated lawsuits that were designed to alter large-scale corporate practices and consumer behaviors relating to products like cigarettes, asbestos, and breast implants. The object of such lawsuits is partly compensation but often it is also social transformation.

Similarly, elaborate injunctive regimes, which were used in the nineteenth and early twentieth century to prevent labor organizing and had similarities to very old judicial practices in areas like probate and bankruptcy, came in the 1960s and 1970s to be applied to public institutions. Often relying on quasi-executive officers called monitors or special masters, courts ran hundreds of public schools, mental hospitals, prisons, housing projects, and other complex organizations. Even sympathetic observers noted that this kind of continuing oversight was not aimed at traditional redress for legal harms but at long-term, open-ended reform.

The courts themselves, either through rulemaking or interpretations of statutes and the Constitution, were responsible for many of these changes. Congress, however, has not legislated to restrain the growth of judicial power except in certain defined areas, such as the labor injunction and prison reform litigation. Significantly, Congress has not amended section 1983 of the Civil Rights Act to limit judicial control over state and local governments. The consequence of judicial assertion and political acquiescence has been a set of changes that have coalesced to create the striking patterns that characterize the modern use of judicial power. The first of these patterns, as intimated in the *Carolene Products* footnote, is a widespread effort by judges to correct deficiencies in the political process.

The school desegregation decision, *Brown v. Board of Education* (1954), powerfully vindicated the idea that the courts should give less deference to political institutions when there is reason to believe that political processes are defective. The Court's determination that racially segregated public schooling is inherently unequal did not directly produce many integrated schools, but it did popularize the view that certain political problems are intractable unless the judiciary intervenes. This view also propelled the courts into a sustained and ambitious campaign to protect freedom of speech from what were seen as the naturally repressive instincts found in the political arena. It fueled an important series of cases attempting to prevent unfair legislative apportionment schemes. It underlay the 1974 decision in the Watergate tapes case—the case, remember, that short-circuited the impeachment process that had begun against President Richard Nixon. And it played a part in the Court's intervention in the 2000 presidential election recount in Florida. The use of judicial power to correct perceived deficiencies in the political process has also helped to produce a freewheeling style of statutory interpretation, through which courts not only fill in important regulatory details, but also sometimes provide meaning that departs from congressional intent. Thus much of the federal statutory law in areas such as racial discrimination in employment and sexual harassment has been supplied by the judiciary.

Since a major function of judicial power now is to resolve issues that it is thought cannot be properly handled in the political process, modern courts cannot follow the model of modesty represented by the *Marbury* decision. Indeed because the divisiveness of an issue is one main reason the political process comes to stalemate, judges must be willing to resolve deeply controversial issues and thus provoke intense opposition. Judges' willingness to face danger during the resistance to school desegregation—or to persevere against administrative resistance to prison reform, or to hold fast against the angry storm provoked by the 1973 decision establishing the right to abortion, or to risk condemnation for resolving issues involving homosexual rights, or to provoke outright defiance by decisions restricting religious behaviors in schools—has become a hallmark of the modern use of judicial power.

The consequences to the nature of judicial power have been varied. State appellate judges to some extent have been attracted to the bold model set by the federal judiciary. The intellectual methods and doctrinal vocabulary used by federal judges have therefore become more influential in the interpretation of state statutes and constitutions. In areas such as the protection of defamatory speech and the establishment of equal funding schemes for public education, some states courts have expanded on federal decisions and thus have intervened more broadly in the political process than have federal judges.

The existence of resistance to controversial judicial decrees has led to an increase in the degree of detail with which courts control political outcomes, a matter to which I will return in the next chapter. Highly specific injunctions—setting, for example, the number of feet of urinal trough that must be provided each prison inmate or the budgetary allotment for a school athletic team—were imposed after resistant administrators failed to respond to more general orders. Similarly, when a court issues an unpopular ruling, political institutions may attempt to achieve their preferred outcomes in new settings. A judicial ruling against classroom prayer, for example, may be met with prayer at school athletic contests. As officials react to judicial rulings and these new policies are challenged, judicial rulings have cumulated and in the aggregate have become increasingly code-like.

Because an important purpose of judicial power in the modern era is to compensate for deficiencies in political and administrative processes, the distinctiveness of legal decision making has become difficult to maintain. The doctrine that some constitutional questions are "political" and unfit for judicial resolution has eroded. More generally, the questions resolved in modern constitutional cases are often indistinguishable from questions traditionally answered by the executive and legislative branches. For example, in a major free speech case the justices considered whether the publication of the *Pentagon Papers* would prolong the war in Vietnam. In 1982, while holding that a state must provide free education to the children of illegal immigrants, they determined that illegal entrants do not impose any significant burden on a state's economy and that undocumented children do not create any special burdens on the educational system. In 1990, the Court held that, in order to pay for an expensive school desegregation plan, a federal trial judge has the authority to set the appropriate level of taxation. Over the years courts have resolved issues about the medical necessity for various abortion regulations, their effect on family life, and so on. It is routine for the judiciary to decide if a state's regulatory interest is important, as well as whether the means chosen for achieving that interest is effective. As the line between political and legal judgment has blurred, judges have felt competent to intervene in a widening array of issues. Thus the exercise of judicial power has become more pervasive, extending to such matters as the discipline of school students and the organization of holiday parades.

Oddly, as the exercise of judicial power has become more ordinary, the justices' claims for exclusive decision-making authority have increased. In its 1992 decision reaffirming the constitutional right to abortion, the Supreme Court referred to itself as speaking "before all others" on constitutional ideals. This claim—that the Court's opinions embody the sovereign voice of the American people and that, therefore, citizens and their officials are obliged to accept the Court's understandings of the Constitution—has appeared with increasing frequency since the courts faced resistance to school desegregation in the 1950s. In a number of cases, involving not only desegregation and abortion but also congressional efforts to prohibit flag burning, enforce the right against self-incrimination, and protect freedom of religion, the Court has treated political disagreement with its decisions as illegitimate.

This drift toward judicial sovereignty on constitutional meaning constitutes a major change in judicial practices. It reverses the tradition of judicial deference to the political branches. It also cuts against the tendency, evident on occasion even during much of the modern era, for the Court to be cautious when faced with intense opposition. In the 1970s, for instance, opposition to the courts' program of busing students to achieve racial balance took diverse and sometimes unseemly forms, from violent street demonstrations to failed proposals in Congress to remove jurisdiction over desegregation cases. Whether in response to this discontent or not, the Court began gradually to restrict the power of lower courts to impose or continue costly remedial programs. There has also been widespread popular dissatisfaction with rulings on the separation of church and state. Recently, the Court has issued a series of decisions on matters like public religious displays and private school vouchers that permit somewhat more interaction between state and religion.

American political life has long been characterized by resistance to judicial decisions. Presidents like Lincoln and Franklin Roosevelt strongly criticized decisions of the Court. Recall that in his campaign for the presidency in 1968 Richard Nixon openly challenged the Warren Court's decisions expanding the rights of criminal defendants. During the New Deal, Congress did not accept restrictive judicial doctrines on the scope of the federal power to regulate commerce. Not long ago Congress enacted legislation that partially challenged the Court's decision invalidating the Religious Freedom Restoration Act as well as its decision invalidating Nebraska's prohibition on "partial-birth abortions." As recently as 2006, the Congress reacted to the Court's decisions on presidential authority in the war on terror by enacting legislation severely limiting judicial authority over unlawful combatants.

Judicial monopolization of constitutional decision making would repudiate the legitimacy of this contentious aspect of American political practice. Nevertheless, to some degree the Court's new claims for the status of its opinions have been accepted during the modern era. Proposals to amend the Constitution in order to reverse the Court's decisions on flag desecration have been repeatedly voted down in the Senate. Congress has declined to enact legislation that would have reversed the Supreme Court's determination about the beginning of human life. Proposals to remove jurisdiction over abortion, school prayer, and school busing have not been enacted, and a bill to restrict the power of federal courts to order tax increases drew little support.

Nevertheless, as we saw in Chapter 1, since about 1970 presidents have sought to nominate individuals to the bench who hold restrained or, at least, temperate views on the judiciary's function, and in reviewing these nominations senators have commonly insisted on such views. While these efforts have possibly reduced the rate of growth of judicial power and certainly have changed some of subjects that occupy the Court's attention, so far the overall role of the Supreme Court in American society and politics has not been significantly reduced.

In many ways, acquiescence to the Court's role is not surprising. That role, and the consequent importance of lower courts throughout the country, is certainly alluring. To judges it offers a prominent, sometimes even heroic, role. To the educated class it promises some direct influence over public policy (since lawyers and judges are members of this class) as well as the indirect advantages that arise from privileging relatively intellectualized forms of argumentation. To members of minority groups it raises the prospect of protection from majoritarian excesses. To everyone it provides some deeply reassuring possibilities, including not only public decision making that appears to be characterized by apolitical rationality but also mandated progress that comes clothed in the language of continuity.

Moreover, at least if legal theorists are to be believed, courts can be expected to identify and modernize deep political traditions, enforce attractive moral principles, improve democratic processes, teach the virtue of tolerance, shake up moribund public institutions, and—all the while—hold society together. Even more exciting is the fact that such hopes and claims are to some degree substantiated by modern American history.

All this is even more alluring because theories of judicial review typically assert that the practice should be highly selective. Alexander Bickel's famous argument that the Court should examine political traditions to identify "enduring values," for example, is coupled with the admonition that constitutional invalidation should be reserved for totally irrational and indefensible legislative acts. Ronald Dworkin, probably the most influential legal theorist of our time, argues for judicial reliance on moral philosophy and urges the Court to identify fundamental moral principles. Possibly the most attractive effort to justify the Warren Court's record, John Hart Ely's "representation reinforcing" model, calls on courts to protect minorities from the kinds of cumulative disadvantages that make normal democratic redress impossible. Many theories apply only to "preferred" constitutional provisions, such as the free speech clause, or to extraordinary circumstances, such as when the social fabric is threatened by irresolvable conflict.

The various versions of exceptionality all mean that judicial interference with normal democratic processes and values can be conceived of as limited and specially justified. Moreover, they carry the bright promise of moral and political clarity. The animating model is the "landmark case," such as *Brown v. Board of Education*, where the Supreme Court strikes a bold, cleansing stroke. Intervening in difficult circumstances on behalf of the highest and best principles, the judiciary rises above political struggle and inertia to achieve powerful lucidity. What was murky or forgotten or ignored or contested is made plain and compelling. Properly chastened and enlightened, political bodies can then carry on with the more ordinary affairs entrusted to them.

It is no wonder, then, that the course on which the Supreme Court is embarked has been so resistant to change. The calls for restraint that echo throughout recent decades of judicial nominations and confirmation hearings sound faint indeed in comparison to the potent forces and ideas that propel the Court on its way. But those faint calls capture a persistent and important recognition that something is seriously amiss in our modern reliance on judicial power.

3

The Consequences of Excess

Much of the inspiration for judicial review in America may have been the landmark case, but the practice certainly has not turned out to be exceptional. The growth of judicial power since 1937 demonstrates that the descent of high constitutional judgment to prosaic coercion occurs in two basic ways. First, the landmark decision itself must be actualized—and this leads to what might be called vertical routinization. The Court made the grand pronouncement that racial segregation in public education is inherently unequal, but then it had to enforce that ruling in innumerable settings. While it is clear enough that segregation mandated by statute is unconstitutional, what of racial imbalances caused by parental choice? By residential segregation? By the school board's reluctance to bus students across town? By teacher training methods? By disparities in athletic programs? As judges are drawn into deciding such questions, they become embroiled in all the problems that face any public administrator—overcoming recalcitrance, sloth, self-interest, and ineptitude. Consequently, judges (or their special masters and monitors) must specify what is required with ever greater particularity. Training manuals must be written, budgets must be set. These same dynamics can be seen in other areas besides school desegregation, notably in the prison reform movement. Courts first announced the high principle that conditions of confinement can themselves amount to cruel and unusual punishment, but in operationalizing this principle they eventually descended to the level of mandating the number of square feet in each cell. Very similar dynamics were at play in the decades after the Supreme Court's landmark pronouncement that abortion in the first two trimesters of pregnancy cannot be made a criminal offense. Next was the question whether states could mandate hospitalization or two-doctor concurrence requirements or parental consent rules or spousal consent rules, and so on.

The second basic reason for the routinization of American judicial review is that the moral force of the landmark decision is difficult to contain—horizontally, so to speak—within the circumstances of the original decision. The principle, being attractive in one setting, naturally seems attractive in other, analogous settings. Equal protection principles, first invoked to determine the fundamental issue of racial segregation, are then applied to more peripheral matters such as gender separation in military academies, zoning rules that disadvantage the retarded, tuition burdens placed on non-citizens, and restrictions on contraceptive distribution to minors. This kind of legal diffusion explains why free speech decisions control not only arguably pivotal issues, like prior restraints on newspaper coverage of the Vietnam War or defamation awards aimed at silencing a civil rights protest movement, but also a vast array of mundane and even tawdry issues arising from public efforts to regulate billboards, profanity, door-to-door solicitation, school dress codes, and automobile license plates. It explains why the fundamental right to privacy was first invoked to insulate married couples from the state but was later applied to contraceptive use by unmarried minors and then to homosexual behavior. Indeed, privacy is used to protect the right of insolvent fathers to remarry and to oversee the provision of medical care to the dying. And the pressure for horizontal expansion explains why the procedures required by due process of law first are said to require legal representation at felony trials but then are used to determine the decision making methods to be used to suspend a student from a public school or to deny public assistance benefits.

I am well aware that both the vertical and horizontal spread of constitutional decision making can be defended. Some or all of the specifications and applications of grand principle can be thought of as important in some way, especially to the individuals affected. It might be possible for a sensitive soul to see something significant in most or maybe even in all governmental contacts with citizens. My point is only that to the degree that courts recognize and respond to perceived injustices pervasively—in ordinary interactions—judicial review no longer can claim the advantages associated with exceptionality. To the degree that judicial interventions become routine, democratic values are correspondingly sacrificed and the potential for special clarity and force is lost. Moreover, as I will attempt to explain next, the pervasive use of judicial power weakens the political culture in ways that encourage continuing and increasing reliance on judicial decision making.

Centralization of Political Discourse

The horizontal spread of the definition of individual rights means, of course, that an increasing array of issues is subject to the Supreme

Court's oversight and thus becomes the subject matter of its opinions. These issues include highly personal and sensitive matters that in the United States were once debated and decided at the state and local level. For instance, the Court's opinions now deal with the nature and significance of specific forms of sexual behavior, with the relationship between husband and wife (as well as between parents and children), with a range of medical procedures (including the grotesque details of certain abortion procedures), and with the specifics of public education (such as the kinds of psychological pressures that exist for adolescents in classrooms and other settings).

The increasing importance of federal judges on matters of immediate importance to people's personal and political lives means that lavish resources are devoted to national judicial discourse. Law schools emphasize national law, of course, and especially national constitutional law. All the best law schools, including those funded and controlled by particular states, define themselves as "national schools." The most successful graduates go to clerk for Supreme Court justices. Books, films, newspaper articles and editorials, and mountains of imaginative scholarship are all directed at evaluating and influencing federal judges. Skilled tacticians are brought in to prepare judicial nominees for their confirmation hearings before the Senate Judiciary Committee, while powerful organizations pour vast resources into investigating the unfortunate nominees' beliefs and personal backgrounds. Eventually, some justices take on celebrity status, either as heroes or villains.

The effect of this concentration of attention and resources is to reduce the vigor of both political and legal discourse at the local level. Suffering the loss of skills and respect that attends second-place finishers in a winner-take-all market, state judges imitate the opinion-writing style of the national judiciary. They often treat their state's own constitutional provisions as if they were indistinguishable from those of the federal Constitution. Similarly, state legislators and executives recognize that they do not have the stature to challenge the Supreme Court's decrees on constitutional or even moral grounds and limply frame their positions as mere variations of policies imposed by the Court. Moreover, because virtually every decision is made against the backdrop of potential judicial review and invalidation, debate about even serious policy making becomes provisional in tone and subordinate in attitude. Perhaps more fundamentally, the capacity of local governments to elicit affection and loyalty from local residents is being undermined. After all, especially beginning in the 1960s local governments became the institutions against which federal courts had to protect people. Frequent judicial interventions, then, have made nearby governments seem vaguely ominous. As decision making at the state and local level becomes less interesting, important, and appealing, even more attention is focused on the national institutions, including, naturally, the judiciary.

Even as the quality of debate and participation at the local level erodes, increased attention to issues at the national level is often unsatisfactory. Insofar as the nationalized issues are being decided by the Court in the arcane language of the law, the public inevitably feels distant from the decision making. But the nationalization of public issues caused by judicial decisions also involves Congress and the president in the same issues, as the political branches react to judicial decisions on issues like partial-birth abortion or gay rights. While the glare generated by the national media and the drama associated with national politicians certainly is colorful, there is also a degeneration of the level of discourse. The decision makers are remote and theatrical. The claims are, as everyone has noticed, often nothing more than exaggerations or sloganeering. More and more of what matters to people is decided far away and in terms that do not seem authentic.

Judicial Methods and the Erosion of Political Self-confidence

Needless to say, the routine resolution of broad arrays of important public issues by the Supreme Court has led to certain adaptations in legal norms. Because the justices' decisions are expected to control the behavior of thousands of public officials and lower court judges, one prevalent opinion-writing technique utilizes an elaborate doctrinal style that is an amalgam of the legalistic and bureaucratic. These three and four part "tests" are designed to signal how categories of cases should be treated and to impart at least the appearance of precision. Their rather bloodless terminology—"rational relationship," "less drastic means," "legitimate interest"—is at once vaguely familiar and yet ultimately arcane. To those citizens who pay attention to the content of the Court's decisions, the doctrines suggest that the justices have access to specialized knowledge and superior methods of analysis. To some degree this impression filters out to the general public and further diminishes confidence in ordinary political decision making. In fact, to a surprising degree doctrinal phrases actually get picked up and used in public debate. Thus a commentator might criticize a proposed abortion regulation as serving only a "legitimate" (as opposed to a "compelling") public purpose, as if there were somewhere a known method for calibrating the importance of the objectives of public policy. Or a city official might fret that a proposed ordinance controlling advertising on city buses would create a "content discrimination," as if it is obviously desirable for government to make no judgments about the value of different types of messages. Citizens, in short, are induced to utilize a language that is mostly foreign to them and to think in a way that is often counter-intuitive and unsatisfactory.

While constitutional doctrines come in many variations, they allow for the invalidation of legislation on the basis of two essential claims: that the public purpose behind the statute is not sufficiently important, or that the means chosen are not closely enough related to the purpose. Now, obviously both the importance and efficacy of a legislative scheme are normally highly controversial matters (a subject to be taken up more fully in Chapter 8). In order to justify the authoritative invalidation of a statute that appears to be aimed at an arguably laudable goal, the Court often must resort to simplification, distortion, and condemnation. Thus, a law designed in part to protect the institution of heterosexual marriage is described by the Supreme Court as wholly unprecedented and inexplicable except on the ground of animosity towards homosexuals. A policy that by its terms permitted both religious and secular invocations at a school event is described as a surreptitious effort to impose prayer. Laws that are expressions of traditional beliefs and practices are disparaged as prejudiced or ignorant.

A second opinion-writing technique that results from the constitutionalization of so much of American politics is unadorned interest balancing. This method, which is less common than doctrinalism but seems to be an emerging trend, abandons both the legalistic and the bureaucratic and substitutes bald, direct claims about instrumental efficacy, human psychology, or morality. In these opinions the Court appears to be participating in ordinary political dialogue, but implicitly (and sometimes explicitly) claims to know more than other decision makers. One side wins because, on balance, its interests are simply more important than the other's. Unadorned interest balancing is a reflection of the normalization of judicial oversight. There is little felt need to resort to established doctrines or other more conventional sources of legal authority because the public is so used to the exercise of judicial review that the justices believe no special justifications are required.

Because unvarnished interest balancing begins by acknowledging that there are legitimate interests on both sides of the case, the task of explaining why the authorities are constitutionally prohibited from favoring one set of those interests is daunting. One tactic is to dramatically elevate the interests favored by the Court, thus exaggerating the dangers posed by the public policy at issue. In an everyday case involving a requirement that door-to-door solicitors register with the local officials before intruding on residents' privacy, the Court worked its concern into a near paroxysm. The offending ordinance, under which approval of the soliciting permit was automatic, was decreed to be offensive "to the very notion of a free society." In even more spectacular language, the Court has famously described restrictions on both the right to abortion and the right to homosexual sodomy as threats to "the right to define one's own concept of existence, of meaning, of the universe and of the mystery of human life." Along with exaggerating the dangers posed by the governmental rule, the Court often deprecates the specific interests the rule protects. In the door-to-door solicitation case the Court recognized that in the abstract privacy in one's home is a significant interest, but the specific problem represented by unwanted solicitors was, said the Court, only an "annoyance." In the sodomy case, the justices admitted that many hold serious moral objections to homosexual conduct, but suggested that those objections somehow lose their force when applied outside an individual's personal ethical code.

What doctrinalism and interest balancing have in common, then, is a tendency to distort and belittle the public's understanding of its own objectives and traditions. This tendency is also characteristic of the third major non-traditional form of constitutional explanation, which is motive analysis. The characterization of legislative motivation was, in more innocent days, avoided on the grounds that the motives behind public enactments are complex and obscure and that, in any event, judicial characterizations would involve undignified inquiries and judgments. However, in modern times, as judicial review has increasingly been seen as essential protection against the constant dangers posed by political institutions, these objections have dropped away. Thus, it is not uncommon for the Court to assert that a public policy is motivated by prejudice or by a desire to establish an official religion or by an intention to suppress a particular point of view. In these cases, the public is rather directly accused of wanting to subvert important and attractive constitutional values.

Traditional sources of legal authority may have their drawbacks, but they have the advantage of permitting a certain dry respect for other decision makers. Using traditional methods, the text of an authoritative constitutional provision might be said (regretfully) to require the invalidation of a perfectly sensible public policy, and the intent behind another provision—outmoded as it arguably is—might (sadly) require the invalidation of a brave piece of social experimentation. But traditional sources of authority have lost some of their force and, in any event, would never convincingly explain the routine application of constitutional law to every imaginable political choice. Consequently, the Court has moved to explanatory techniques thought to be more sophisticated and also adequate to the rather substantial task at hand. The difficulty is that these techniques often reflect back on the public a distorted and mean-spirited view of its values and purposes. To the extent that segments of the public dutifully accept this view, political self-confidence and self-respect are eroded. And many, distrustful of the foolish, dangerous people that are apparently in charge of political institutions, turn anxiously back to the Court.

Quite aside from how judicial opinions are framed, the deep commitment of lawyers and judges to the idea of the landmark case saps the public's confidence. Many, many Americans—and certainly most lawyers—are convinced that public school segregation ended only because of *Brown v. Board of Education*. When careful historical work indicates that *Brown* itself led to almost no desegregation in the south and that the eventual desegregation that did take place appears to be attributable to the Civil Rights Act of 1964, the work is either ignored or rationalized on the ground that the Civil Rights Act must have been caused by *Brown*. When evidence indicates that the Civil Rights Act was caused largely by northern sympathy for the plight of civil rights protesters, this evidence is rationalized on the ground that the civil rights protests must have been caused by *Brown*. When no evidence for this proposition can be found, the acolytes of *Brown* resort to mere assertion and faith: *Brown must have caused desegregation in ways that the empirical evidence just does not pick up.* One need not resolve the complex questions of social causality involved in this dispute, nor insist that *Brown* played no part at all in the grand struggle for desegregation. But it does seem that in this debate there is a strange resistance to the possibility that the American people—in Congress or on the streets—played a significant role in overcoming one of the nation's deepest injustices. The self-importance of the legal profession thus works against a proper recognition of the decency of the American people.

A different kind of damage to political self-confidence is sharply illustrated by another successful landmark decision, *United States v. Nixon*, the famous Watergate tapes case that was decided in 1974. Recall that President Richard Nixon's illegal schemes and his notorious cover-up threatened the legitimacy of the office of the presidency. Political chaos seemed possible as Congress prepared for impeachment hearings. The Court's hurried decision, requiring Nixon to turn over the Watergate tapes to a grand jury, and the president's subsequent resignation truncated the impeachment process. The public understandably saw the *Nixon* case as re-establishing political order and the rule of law. Like *Brown*, it is one of the most admired opinions of all time.

The long-term consequences of *Nixon*, however, are sobering. For one thing, the decision broke down the long-established political practice that permitted the president to keep Oval Office communications confidential. In exposing the president to the power of a grand jury, it led to the later decision that exposed President Clinton (and, of course, future presidents as well) to the power of trial judges and even private attorneys seeking information in civil cases. This subordination of the president to the judicial branch is by itself problematic, at least for those who believe there is a need for an energetic executive branch. But, more generally, by insisting that the prosecutorial needs of the grand jury were more important than presidential confidentiality, the Court in *United States v. Nixon* planted a new and deeply troublesome idea—namely, that it is constitutionally unacceptable to rely on the president and the attorney general to make decisions about prosecuting high executive officials. By the same token, it legitimated the idea that impeachment and other political sanctions for executive wrongdoing are untrustworthy and insufficient.

These ideas were later institutionalized in the law establishing the office of Independent Counsel, a law that the Court eventually and surprisingly found to be a constitutional intrusion into presidential control over the executive branch. Even when this law expired, the impulse it embodied lived on, as is evidenced by the periodic establishment by the Justice Department of independent prosecutors. (A recent, grim example is Patrick Fitzgerald and his prolonged pursuit of White House aide Lewis Libby for lying about the "outing" of Valerie Plame as a CIA agent.) The Court's effort in *Nixon* to restore order to the political system and to enshrine "the rule of law" led, then, to the displacement of politics and the bureaucratization of the prosecutorial function. Political judgment was replaced by professionalized norms and a kind of legalistic perfectionism. Presidents ever since have been beset by accusations and investigations.

Possibly the worst of all worlds was achieved when these trends came to fruition in the earnest and conscientious person of Kenneth Starr. Precisely because he was entirely true to his statutory duties, his investigation derailed a presidency and his report triggered the impeachment of President William Clinton. But because Starr's statutory role was at its root predicated on distrust of both politics and impeachment, neither the country nor the Senate could summon the will to provide a full trial or to exercise high political judgment. The "trial" was a staged drama, and the debate on both sides was dominated by legalized arguments designed to permit senators to evade personal responsibility for their decisions. In attempting to enforce the rule of law and to circumvent the uncertainties of political struggle, *United States v. Nixon* thus eventually resulted in an astonishing combination of distortions in our constitutional system: simultaneously, the depletion of the constitutional office of the presidency and the depletion of the process constitutionally mandated for keeping him in line. It takes political self-confidence to rely on publicly accountable mechanisms to restrain executive wrongdoing, and self-confidence is exactly what the Court undermined by taking on the role of hero in *United States v. Nixon*.

The Institutionalization of Political Revenge

The resignation of President Nixon and the impeachment of President Clinton are signs of a dangerous shift in American political life. For almost two centuries prior to Nixon's departure from office, no president had been driven from office during his term, despite wars, economic crises, illnesses and scandals. The only other president to have been impeached was Andrew Johnson back in 1868. But twice in less than thirty years we have experienced seismic attacks on presidents. Even this does not tell the whole story, for three modern presidents (Gerald Ford, Jimmy Carter, and the first George Bush) were so weakened at the end of their first terms that they could not win re-election, while one (Lyndon Johnson) did not even run for a second term. Presidents Johnson, Ford, Reagan, and George W. Bush (the younger) were all severely criticized for alleged abuses of power. The assault on Reagan over Iran-Contra was so severe that his attorney general feared impeachment. And the administration of George W. Bush is regularly depicted as illegitimate (a state of affairs to which I will return in Chapter 9). In short, the twin engines that drove the Watergate crisis—political unpopularity and serious charges of impropriety—have become the norm in recent years.

Presidential unpopularity and impropriety, needless to say, did not suddenly appear in the past few decades. In modern times presidential politics has taken on new levels of bitterness, and there is a new willingness to destabilize that office. One explanation is the way that the two trends just discussed—the nationalization of moral issues and the professionalization of presidential oversight—interact. As the Supreme Court has been busily and insistently nationalizing a range of sensitive issues, presidents have been forced to take stands that conflict with some citizens' deepest moral and religious beliefs. Much of the emotional fuel that sets loose the relentless prosecutorial machine arises from the resulting cultural symbolism that attaches to the office.

Nixon, for instance, was hated by the intellectual elite—embodied in Archibald Cox—partly because his "Southern strategy" challenged the moral leadership of the Supreme Court on criminal justice and, to a degree, school desegregation. Some of the energy for the drive to remove President Clinton from office came from citizens embittered by the elite's control (through the judiciary) over issues like flag burning and gay rights. Moreover, Mr. Clinton's crisis was in part payback for Nixon's demise (in which Mrs. Clinton had a minor part) and for the ugly campaign against Robert Bork's nomination to the high court. Cultural conservatives see these events as flashpoints where formal disenfranchisement and prosecutorial harassment intersect. The impeachment of President Clinton, in turn, surely is being repaid in the repeated claim that the presidency of George W. Bush is illegitimate. Bush supporters will, no doubt, lie in wait to undermine the next Democratic president.

One of the unsung triumphs of our constitutional system is the tradition of stable presidential terms. It is truly sobering that Americans now are close to taking the drive for political revenge so far as to imperil this tradition. This recklessness, however, is only the most prominent sign of a deep polarization that is degrading political life. Excessive judicial power is certainly not the only cause of political animosity and institutional instability, but it is one cause.

Legal Instability and Political Anxiety

It is sometimes asserted, at least by certain legal scholars, that the judiciary is successful in providing the kind of stable legal meanings that allow for predictability and a sense of security. However, as I shall show in the next chapter, others who are less encumbered with high theory have an uneasy sense that the Court's constitutional and statutory interpretations are changing, perhaps effectively amending, our laws. In fact, on occasion it is not hard to see palpable evidence of an unhealthy anxiety created by doubts about whether judges are faithful to the words that express the public's will.

Let us go back to 2000 when the Supreme Court stopped the recount that was underway in the Florida presidential election. At the time, it was natural to believe that the justices had once again saved us from political and legal disaster. There is no doubt that the Florida Supreme Court's stunning decision to order manual recounts across Florida created the specter of chaos, as Chief Justice Wells of the Florida Supreme Court said in dissent. Something was disturbing in these events that went beyond uncertainty about presidential succession. What the Florida decision did was to demonstrate how legal argumentation in America has metastasized. When even the plainest meaning is subject to the relentless pressure exerted by all the urgent words streaming from the mouths of lawyers, our institutions are exposed to something close to intellectual anarchy.

To get a clear view of the nature of that chaos, one detail from the Florida court's opinion can be extracted. In its first decision, the court had said that Secretary of State Katherine Harris had abused her discretion by enforcing the seven-day statutory deadline for certifying the vote, and it instructed her to observe a twelve-day deadline. In their new decision, the four Florida justices concluded that the secretary had abused her discretion by enforcing the court's *own* twelve-day deadline.

If words like "seven" and "twelve" cannot hold, nothing can hold and uncertainty stretches away to the horizon. Touchingly oblivious to the anarchical implications of its own opinion, the Florida court simply assumed that the manual recount could proceed in an orderly and timely fashion. In fact, of course, everything was thrown up in the air. Before the United States Supreme Court stayed the recount, lawyers were arguing before a trial judge about the procedures for conducting the recounts. Those determinations might have been appealed. The recounted vote itself might have been challenged, and that determination might have been appealed. The Florida legislature could have nullified the recount by statute, but that statute could have led to a lawsuit and an appeal. In counting the electoral votes, Congress eventually would have resolved the uncertainty, but if words like "seven" and "twelve" do not hold, the congressional count could be questioned in court and any decision appealed, and so on until it is time for another presidential election.

It is understandable, then, that many felt relief that the United States Supreme Court re-established order by permanently halting the recount. But there is irony, and eventually perhaps futility, in using the lawyers who sit on the Supreme Court to stabilize what lawyers and lower courts had destabilized. After all, in recent decades the Court itself has done much to establish the very judicial role that the four Florida justices embraced so heedlessly. To take the most prominent example, it announced a right to abortion when not a word in the Constitution can be found on that subject. It also converted into an authorization for racial preferences a federal statute whose plain words and ascertainable purpose prohibited racial discrimination. Through "interpretation" it grafted a complicated sexual harassment code onto a federal law that was silent on that specific subject. Indeed, as we shall see in Chapter 4, it is arguable that the modern Supreme Court's basic role has been to alter established legal understandings and to open up vast panoramas of adversarial argument.

In fact, *Bush v. Gore* itself may well put in motion a chain of destabilization. At the least, the imposition of equal protection standards on state ballot counting procedures has dizzying potential for generating lawsuits. If the Court had not ruled decisively against the recount, the legal chaos in Florida would have been ended by the Florida legislature and by Congress. In the long run a non-judicial solution might have led to constitutional stability. What we can know is that in the year 2000 the anxious sense that words had lost their meaning was the result of a state court following the intellectual model established by decades of Supreme Court innovations.

Judicial Power and Defiance

Although, as I have said, Americans tend to honor law and courts and to accept dutifully the Supreme Court's bleak depictions of political decision making, just about every kind of group on the political spectrum at one time or another stands up and expresses fury at the Court. It is an odd but true fact that when Americans are not marching hopefully towards the Supreme Court building for protection and vindication, they are likely to be loudly decrying the judiciary's hubris and illegitimacy. This distrust and anger takes many forms—from outraged academic and journalistic commentary, to laws aimed at inducing the Court to reverse itself, to sullen and sometimes violent street-level resistance.

The reasons for this vehement, if episodic and ambivalent, opposition go far beyond the distortive and contemptuous messages conveyed by modern constitutional decisions. One additional reason is that the more detailed and pervasive the application of constitutional law becomes the more implausible the underlying constitutional interpretations become. Supreme Court decisions are notorious for strained, if not downright inaccurate, accounts of American constitutional and political history, for wildly inconsistent applications of—as well as statements of—doctrine, of casual treatment of text, and for unsubstantiated assertions about highly contested matters. It is true that when judicial review was used more sparingly, even the occasional decision could be intellectually weak. But the task of credible explanation has become more difficult as the Court has had more to explain. Moreover, as long as Supreme Court decisions are exceptional, it is at least possible to draw on the mythic status of the fundamental law. But when that law is found to be relevant to everyday affairs, to that degree it cannot seem special or basic. Everything, after all, cannot be fundamental.

A second reason for public dissatisfaction is that the routine application of constitutional law makes possible whole programs of law reform litigation. Consider the model for the modern practice of judicial review, the school desegregation litigation. This campaign began by attacking provable inequalities in specific school systems and by degrees moved to an attack in principle on racial segregation in public schools and ended as a revolutionary assault on the whole system of racial caste in the American South. As laudable as this revolution was, the notion that grew out of it was that it is generally desirable for society to be vulnerable to revolutionary change imposed by distant and somewhat alien figures on the basis of rather inaccessible legal arguments and theories generated by academics and litigators. The possibility of this kind of sweeping, uncontrollable change comes to seem omnipresent because legal theories work from small victories to larger principles. Thus virtually any of the unexpected decisions that the Court hands down every year could eventually flower into a vast program of social change. For example, a few years ago the Court offered homosexuals what appeared to be an extremely narrow constitutional protection against discrimination. The law reform theories that went into this decision, however, were aimed at nothing less than cultural transformation, including eventually the transformation of the institution of marriage. Not long ago, posting another victory for these theories, the Court elevated homosexual sodomy to an exalted constitutional freedom—all the while sternly denying that this elevation threatened marriage or other important social institutions. No one, of course, can know whether this denial will hold. Segments of the public, however, already feel anxiously vulnerable to cultural transformations to which they have not consented and cannot control. For these people, whatever the Court finally decides on the right of homosexuals to marry, there is already a significantly enhanced sense of uneasiness and powerlessness that readily translates into anger. The resulting efforts to protect against judicially imposed transformations—efforts like state anti-gay rights initiatives or the proposed federal constitutional amendment prohibiting gay marriage—frighten and enrage the groups who occupy the other side of the cultural divide. Demands become more strident, as distrust and anxiety increase all around.

Of course, disagreement on issues like abortion, gay rights, and public expression of religious belief would exist independently of the Court's constitutional decisions. But these decisions resolve such issues by imposing rules that are explicit, highly rationalized, uniform, ostensibly permanent, and national. Thus, the Court removes many of the opportunities that otherwise would exist for softening conflict. After the Court issues an opinion, it is more difficult for members of the public to ignore or suppress an issue. It is harder to construct compromises. It is virtually impossible for groups to find refuge in low-visibility localized rules. Consequently, those who were disinterested can be mobilized. Those who were interested become inflamed. Those who were inflamed become fanatical. The middle, as in the abortion debate, drops from sight.

It is against this turbulent backdrop that the justices decide how to react to opposition to their decisions. Consider their perspective. They do not see their use of power as unusual or in need of special justification because they are by now used to settling highly contentious issues. Because they see their use of power as ordinary, they expect compliance. Moreover, through the decades of pervasive judicial review a massive outpouring from the most eminent law professors at the best national law schools attests to the importance and legitimacy of their actions. Elite opinion makers in the most respected newspapers and the most intellectual radio networks extol their landmark decisions as heroic, essential, path-breaking. In contrast, the rhetoric of the justices' own opinions depicts political decision makers as irrational, prejudiced, and dangerous to the Republic. The intellectual frame encouraged by their own work, therefore, tends to strip the positions of opponents of their moral seriousness. Conflict and disagreement become inexplicable or downright pernicious. The justices, therefore, are not only startled by opposition, but deeply dismayed.

While the justices conceive of their decisions as representing a kind of enlightened progress, they also understand them to be interpretations of a permanent, fundamental law. Consequently, they resist seeing their work as destabilizing or anxiety-provoking to those whose ways of life are being upset. The vociferousness of the opposition, as a result, seems even more puzzling and sinister. The protests, after all, are directed against what the justices depict as deep principles long central to the American system.

For all their certitude, the justices are beset by a certain kind of doubt as well. The reasoning in many decisions is, in fact, strained and unconvincing if not outright implausible. The justices not only know this but also know that the old idea of law as logically demonstrable deductions is inadequate to their modern role. This means that even the best reasoning, as right as it may seem to the justices, is not ineluctable. Along with their extreme sense of institutional importance, then, the justices are subject to an intense sense of limitation and even futility. The opposition should be convinced, the justices feel sure, but ultimately there is no to way accomplish that. Where persuasion stops, brute authority must be invoked.

For a number of reasons, then, pervasive judicial review has generated angry criticism of the Supreme Court and sometimes opposition to its decrees. Paradoxically, however, this fervor seems on the whole only to encourage more extreme and strident claims of judicial authority. This reaction is a result of the psychological and intellectual context created by the routine exercise of judicial power. That context causes the justices to perceive conflict in the political arena as profoundly dangerous, even anarchic. The Court's role, then, is understood to be profoundly important. The justices believe that their constitutional decisions prevent political and cultural chaos, and, accordingly, they see disagreement with those decisions as truly threatening. Therefore, they react to the resistance their decisions engender by exercising more power over public policy and by making more authoritarian demands for public compliance.

There is no doubt that American judicial review has sometimes been a useful, even an admirable, practice. It has on important occasions vindicated high ideals. But the full picture should be troubling to everyone. Excessive judicial power has accelerated other trends towards political centralization while it has subverted traditional legal norms. As a consequence, it has weakened and demoralized politics at the state and local level at the same time that it has exacerbated cultural and political divisions. More troubling yet, the cultural and political damage done by judicial review works in a way that only fuels greater and more authoritarian uses of judicial power. This ratchet-like effect is not as perverse as it might at first seem. The judiciary is, after all, a part of the political culture and ultimately expresses the character of the people in that culture. Dependence on problem solving by the courts is an indication of the American people's simultaneous perfectionism and self-doubt. To the extent that judicial review operates to enhance these traits it is generating the conditions for its own expansion.

4

Thinking like a Lawyer

While Americans are deeply fascinated by and attracted to a practice that does serious political and cultural damage, they are also uneasy about it. Judicial confirmation hearings, although sometimes derided as ritualized and insincere, do convey this sense of unease and also the types of reassurances provided by the nominees. Indeed, since the nominees to the Supreme Court are all prominent and successful lawyers, their reassurances can be profitably examined to see whether the legal mind is capable of conceiving of a different course for the Court.

A baseline for this inquiry is provided by the confirmation hearings for William J. Brennan, Jr. in 1957. Like Chief Justice Earl Warren (who had been appointed a few years earlier), Brennan was a Republican nominee. He was a graduate of Harvard Law School and had been a prominent lawyer and judge in New Jersey. His hearings are the place to start partly because three years previously the Court had decided *Brown v. Board of Education*. While today *Brown* is the emblem of the heroic use of judicial power, at the time it was widely criticized for, among other things, attributing a meaning to the equal protection clause that its authors had not intended. The scope of the criticisms generated by *Brown* can be appreciated by noting the content of a prestigious lecture (the Holmes Lecture) delivered at Harvard Law School not long after Brennan's nomination. At this event Herbert Wechsler, one of the most eminent legal scholars of the time, argued that *Brown* lacked an elemental characteristic of lawfulness, that is, an explanation for the outcome that the justices would be willing to use in other cases. *Brown*, then, had raised serious questions about the nature of law and the role of the Court.

These questions were certainly not fully vented in the hearings, but they did make a veiled appearance when a senator asked Brennan whether it was a sound rule of construction that the Constitution has a fixed and definite meaning. The nominee, who would in later years be the most able and persistent advocate of a "living constitution," declined to give a straightforward answer. He said, "I don't know ... that I could answer that question categorically." Later, however, Brennan was asked whether the Supreme Court could amend the Constitution, and he gave a strong answer. The "only way," to amend the Constitution, said Brennan, is through the procedures laid out in Article V of that document.

Now, consider what is at stake in these apparently unremarkable exchanges. The very idea of constitutionalism requires that some basic rules remain stable over time. Relative permanence, after all, is one thing that distinguishes a constitutional rule from a statutory requirement or an administrative policy. So when Brennan was unwilling to say that the Constitution has a fixed meaning, he might have been thought to be challenging a basic supposition of our constitutional system. Indeed, he might have been thought to be challenging the very idea of a written constitution as law.

The usual response to this problem is to distinguish between, on the one hand, an interpretive change, which is depicted as a change that adapts but remains true to some more permanent meaning, and, on the other, an amendment. As long as the Court is interpreting rather than amending, the idea of constitutionalism remains in tact. That is one reason Brennan so flatly denied that the Court could amend our fundamental legal charter.

The distinction between interpretation and amendment is therefore crucial. At the same time that we are deeply dependent on judicial decisions like *Brown* that alter basic legal norms, the distinction enables Americans to believe that we live under a Constitution and that the Court is also subject to that Constitution. Alternatively, if modern legal thought is unable to distinguish between interpretation and amendment, Americans must live with the possibility that the justices are amending the Constitution in the course of ordinary adjudication. Recognizing this risk would generate deep problems for a people whose national identity is tied so closely to constitutional ideals and whose history insists that sovereignty to define those ideals rests with the people.

In 1957 Brennan did not attempt to explain the difference between changes created by interpretation and those that can be accomplished only through amendment. Sixteen years later in a case called *Frontiero v. Richardson*, he wrote an opinion (which did not have enough support to represent the official position of the Court) arguing that the principle of equal protection of the laws should be understood to protect against gender discrimination in the same way that it protects against racial discrimination. At that very moment, the equal rights amendment, which was designed to achieve this same change, was pending before the states pursuant to the amendment procedures set out in Article V.

Was Justice Brennan proposing to use interpretation to amend the Constitution? Not necessarily. It could be that the equal rights amendment (ERA) was based on a mistaken belief that the Constitution did not already treat discrimination against women the same as discrimination against blacks. This mistaken belief would have been understandable because, until Justice Brennan's opinion in 1973, no justice had recognized that the two forms of discrimination had equivalent constitutional status. So, what would have been less understandable is how so many justices could have misinterpreted the Constitution for so long.

In *Frontiero*, then, Justice Brennan had an opportunity to supply the answer that he did not offer the Senate Judiciary Committee in 1957. Especially because Justice Powell wrote that Brennan's position was inappropriate in light of the amendment process that was underway, Brennan might have responded by explaining the difference between interpretation and amendment. His opinion does not specifically address this question, but it does provide strong indications as to what kinds of considerations Justice Brennan thought to be relevant to judicial interpretation. His opinion canvasses American history to conclude that gender discrimination had been used to put women "not on a pedestal, but in a cage...." In fact, it goes further to assert that throughout the nineteenth century the status of women was "comparable to that of blacks under the pre-Civil War slave codes." It dismisses the legal significance of recent improvements in the position of women. And it offers the judgment that gender characteristics usually bear "no relation to ability to perform or contribute to society."

Some of the claims in Brennan's opinion are conventional wisdom today. This, however, should not obscure the grand scale of his analysis. That analysis is nothing short of a definitive characterization of the place of women in American history and the present significance of gender differences. Moreover, his was certainly not an uncontroversial characterization. Needless to say, throughout our history many Americans firmly believed (or assumed) that gender distinctions in the law often reflected love and concern and that such differences were highly relevant to one's place in society. Brennan's equation of the treatment of women with the treatment of slaves was an interesting argument, but it certainly represented a radical shift in cultural understanding. Even in the 1970s public attitudes apparently had not moved that far because the ERA was fervently opposed and never ratified.

Justice Brennan may have been convinced that his position in *Frontiero* on gender discrimination could be distinguished from a constitutional amendment. Or he may have harbored the idea that the only difference between interpretation and amendment is the procedure through which the change is made. If so, it is no wonder he did not address the issue, since that position would mean that the Court can do through interpretation anything that the American people can do through amendment. What is clear is that he assumed that a judicial interpretation of the Constitution could take into account, and resolve, the most sweeping historical and social issues. He thought it a legal issue to be determined by the justices whether the entire history of legal distinctions based on gender was essentially benign or malignant, and he thought it a legal issue to decide whether gender is generally relevant to social roles. These are matters of fundamental national aspiration and cultural self-understanding. If interpretation and amendment overlap to this degree, senators would be well advised to push harder than they did with nominee Brennan to find out just where the judicial power to interpret ends.

A Record of Judicial Amendment?

Today the suspicion that the power of judicial review is used to amend the Constitution is difficult to keep submerged. For one thing, in the modern era the Court has frequently announced major new departures. Besides the right to racially desegregated schools, which did not emerge until 1954, consider that school prayer was not declared to be unconstitutional until 1962. "One person/one vote" was not mandated until 1964, the same year that defamation laws were first thought to raise free speech problems. *Miranda* warnings were first thought to be constitutionally required in 1966. The Court did not begin its campaign against gender discrimination until 1971. Patronage systems began to raise free speech problems only in 1976, and flag burning was not constitutionally protected until 1989. Homosexual sodomy became a protected liberty interest in 2003. Every one of these decisions, and many more, announced striking new understandings of the meaning of the Constitution, and every one is difficult to justify in terms of the intended meaning of the document. This does not necessarily mean that none of the decisions can be justified or that the distinction between interpretation and amendment has broken down. But the fact of constant innovation during the modern era does make it more difficult to cling to a belief in the Constitution as a fundamental law that expresses the sovereign will of the people. Even if the Court's belabored explanations have some plausibility, observers are left wondering why it took the justices so long to come to their newly announced interpretations.

Listing specific innovations does not capture the significance and scale of the changes introduced by the Supreme Court. The Constitution, a rather short document that is concerned mainly with setting up certain decision making structures, has been transformed, as we saw in the last chapter, into a lengthy, detailed set of prescriptions that resolve all manner of moral and political disputes. Some of the principles used to resolve these disputes, such as the right to privacy, do not appear anywhere in the text of the document and are said to be inferred from political practices or moral calculations. To a degree, then, a written charter has been changed into an unwritten one.

Moreover, modern interpretations have changed basic priorities. Property, which the founders thought highly important, is given little protection, while sexual freedom, with which they did not concern themselves, is given powerful protections. A Bill of Rights that was originally seen as protecting against federal power is now mainly used to limit state governments. A national government that was undoubtedly intended to have only limited regulatory power is now permitted to exercise, for all practical purposes, unlimited power. And today the president, who was originally vested with "the executive power," is forbidden by laws said by the Court to be constitutional to control the leadership of a vast array of administrative agencies. Everyday facts of political life, then, make it difficult to suppress the suspicion that even the basic governmental structure set out in the original compact has been significantly altered through interpretation.

Political Anxiety about the Changing Constitution

Americans, it must be said, have watched all these changes in their fundamental law with remarkable equanimity. Except when a particular outcome offends a segment of the population, most people seem to take pride in the fact that they live under the Constitution that the country's gifted founders wrote while at the same time also accepting the notion that the constant alterations are just the work of judges trying to keep those glorious first principles up to date. Nevertheless, since 1970 the politicians who make up the Senate Judiciary Committee do rather consistently express an underlying unease.

This anxiety takes the form of repeated questions posed to nominees to the Court about matters that might seem, at least to a naïve person, unnecessary (or perhaps even insulting) when confirming someone to the nation's highest court of law. The question put to Brennan back in 1957 about whether the Court can amend the Constitution was repeated not only to Burger in 1970 but in subsequent years to Blackmun, Rehnquist, Stevens, and Ginsburg. All the nominees were asked variations on related questions: whether the words of the Constitution bind the justices, whether judges are permitted to legislate, and whether decisions should be based on personal preferences.

Neither the senators nor the nominees, however, were naïve; all understood the ideas of law and interpretation as they are presented in the nation's law schools and as they are utilized in legal arguments in courtrooms across the land. Confirmation hearings are political theater in some respects, but for the most part they provide a reasonably faithful exposition of how modern lawyers think.

Indeed, even the relatively rare occasions when nominees do depart from mainstream legal thinking are instructive about the contours of the modern lawyer's mind. These deviations tend to involve testimony that is simple and strong but completely implausible to legally-trained observers. As I indicated earlier, for example, when Burger was asked whether the Constitution has a "fixed, definite meaning," he did not, as Brennan had, avoid a clear answer. He maintained that the words of the Constitution are "very plain words" and should be given their plain meaning. Now, the overwhelming consensus among law professors and practicing lawyers is that important constitutional phrases like "due process of law" and "freedom of speech" and "equal protection of the law" are not at all plain. In fact, Justice Black's quirky insistence to the contrary, which was the model for Warren Burger's later answers, was rationalized by one law professor as a kind of well-intentioned myth that Black must have known to be false.

At any rate, while most nominees have testified that the words of the Constitution bind the justices, few have claimed that the words have plain meaning. One who did, Harry Blackmun, eventually wrote the opinion establishing a constitutional right to abortion. Whatever the merits of that opinion might be, no one would argue that it derives the right to abortion from plain constitutional text. Robert Bork's opposition to the reasoning in the abortion opinion was a main basis for the charge by highly respected legal scholars that he was outside the legal mainstream. Blackmun, whatever his answers while being confirmed, eventually found the mainstream.

Recognizing that the words of the Constitution are at least sometimes not clear or plain is the dominant and sophisticated position in legal thinking today, but this recognition presents an obvious problem. If the words of the Constitution are not plain—if they are general or obscure or complex—how are judges bound by them? What is to keep the justices from attributing to those words a meaning that reflects the justice's own personal preferences or philosophical commitments? Virtually all the nominees since 1970, even while maintaining that text is only a starting point, have denied that personal beliefs or preferences should determine constitutional meaning.

To take an extreme example, in 1971 William Rehnquist was asked whether there is any room in interpretation to interject a judge's personal views. Rehnquist's answer, like Burger's earlier answer on whether the constitutional text has a fixed meaning, was admirably blunt and brief: "None," he said. Predictably, this absolute answer is also sharply at odds with modern legal thinking. In fact, the answer was so implausible by modern standards that Rehnquist himself later abandoned it. He said (somewhat ungrammatically), "[T]here is no doubt in my mind that each of us ... take to the Court what I am at the present time. There is no escaping it." With respect to the broad phrasing of the due process clause, the source of the right to abortion, Rehnquist continued, "I will try to divorce my personal views as to what I thought it ought to mean from what I conceived the framers to have intended."

Notice that what Rehnquist ended up saying was that a judge *cannot* interpret entirely independently from personal experiences and beliefs and that the main constraint against substituting a justice's views for those who ratified the Constitution is the justice's own effort. This is what is taught in law schools, and it is what most lawyers believe. Many other nominees, including, for example, Blackmun, Stevens, O'Connor, Souter, and Roberts, said much the same in their hearings. But the admission that personal preferences cannot be entirely escaped inevitably reinvigorates doubts about whether the justices are amending the Constitution to suit their own inclinations.

In 1986 when Rehnquist again went before the Judiciary Committee, this time to be confirmed as chief justice, he found that Senator Biden was wondering about this very problem. In fact, Biden raised it in the context of the same issue raised by Justice Brennan's opinion in *Frontiero*, using the principle of equal protection to protect women from discrimination. Biden posited that the equal protection clause had been enacted in order to protect blacks from discrimination and asked how extending it to protect women from discrimination could be justified. More specifically, he asked whether extending even some minimal protection from discrimination to women—as Rehnquist had voted to do in 1971—was not changing, rather than interpreting, the Constitution. And he pressed ahead to offer a possible response to the question that Justice Brennan had not answered in his *Frontiero* opinion: if the Court could protect all races under the same standard that is used to protect blacks, why could the Court not also extend that same level of protection to women?

Accurately noting that interpretive decisions (such as whether to protect races other than the black race and whether to protect women and what level of protection to afford either) were not "written into the fourteenth amendment," Biden concluded that all these judgments involved changing the Constitution. Even Rehnquist, then, was committed to a "living Constitution." And then Biden lowered the boom. Since these are all interpretative judgments that change the meaning of the document, Rehnquist could not criticize others, like Brennan, who wanted to go further than did Rehnquist in protecting women. He could not criticize them for "tampering" with intended meaning because "[y]ou tamper as much as they tamper, right?"

In this exchange, Senator Biden was in effect supplying the radical answer to the question whether interpretation can be distinguished from amendment. He was suggesting that every member of the Court who ever departs from intended meaning, including the conservative Justice Rehnquist, is effectively amending the Constitution. This comes close to saying that interpretation as practiced by the modern Court *is* amendment except that the Court changes the Constitution by resolving cases rather than the through procedures laid out in Article V.

Rehnquist's arresting reply was to distinguish his own interpretations from those of people [perhaps like Brennan] that say "everything that bothers them should be [unconstitutional]."[1] So, Rehnquist was insisting that personal preferences play a part in interpretation, but there must be limits. Not everything a justice dislikes is unconstitutional. Biden persisted. "But do you not … in fact reject things you dislike? … [D]o you not apply your philosophy as to the role of women in society to how you read that amendment?" The beleaguered Justice Rehnquist answered, "[Y]ou cannot get away from your philosophy … as judge. But I think a judge should make a conscious effort not to simply bring his own philosophies."

---

1.   In context, Rehnquist probably meant unconstitutional in the same way as discrimination against blacks is unconstitutional.

Rehnquist's answers suggest that, in addition to whatever assurance is provided by a justice's effort to restrain the role of personal preferences in assigning meaning to the Constitution, there is a safeguard against judicial amendment if the justice looks to something other than personal preference. (Look again at his words: "a conscious effort not to simply bring his own philosophies.") One might think that this is such a slim source of assurance of lawfulness that it must have been a slip of the tongue. Can it be that Rehnquist believed that the difference between interpretation and amendment is that in interpretation the judge tries not to be guided *wholly* by personal preferences? For those who would dismiss the particular words used by Rehnquist, it should be a sobering fact that very similar phrasing turns up in the confirmation hearings of several other nominees. David Souter, for instance, distanced himself from deriving legal standards "based simply on personal judicial views of what would be desirable in the world" and later noted that justices should "repress a level of purely personal choice." Similarly, Antonin Scalia denied that it would be acceptable to ascribe to the Constitution "whatever content the current times seem to require." Anthony Kennedy said that judges cannot issue "any decree necessary to achieve a just society." And Samuel Alito assured the assembled senators that the Supreme Court is "not free to do anything it wants."

These answers are important, I think, as indications of the nominees' perceptions about the depth of senators' concerns. The phrasing is responsive to the tacit question, *can judges just do anything they want?* However, like the claims that constitutional text is plain and that personal philosophies should play no role in judicial decision making, these answers are sufficiently straightforward and strong to flag them as departures from mainstream legal thinking. Sophisticated lawyers would not concede that a justice is interpreting, rather than amending, the Constitution as long as personal preference or philosophy is not the whole basis of the decision. The standard view about the role of personal belief in judging—the view held by most lawyers and legal educators—is that something more is required to justify a judicial act as interpretation. What these additional requirements are is somewhat complicated, as the confirmation hearings repeatedly demonstrate.

Combining Realism and Formalism

Under the dominant idea of the judicial role, the realistic acknowledgment that judges cannot completely escape their own experiences and values when deciding cases is matched with the more formalistic demand that judges also base their interpretations on sources that are thought to be conventionally legal and external to the judge. Nominee Breyer exemplified this approach when he said that justices are bound by "the words, the history, the precedents, the traditions…" as did Alito when he referred to "objective things" like text, history, and precedent. Kennedy was more expansive in saying that the constitutional meaning of privacy should be determined by deciding "the essentials of the right to human dignity, the injury to the person, … the anguish to the person, the inability of the person to manifest his or her own personality, [and] the inability of the person to obtain his or her own self-fulfillment…." When Senator Grassley rather reasonably responded that "[t]he problem with this theory is that every justice's concept of human dignity is very personal…," Kennedy replied that judges are guided by "the text and the purpose of the Constitution…." "We are not," he affirmed, basing decisions on "our own subjective beliefs." Thus reference to traditional legal materials can discipline even the most expansive moral inquiries.

It might be objected that invoking multiple sources of legal authority only makes matters worse. If it was naïve for Burger and Rehnquist to think that plain words could constrain judges, how does it help to add additional layers of words? After all, legal precedents consist of wordy judicial opinions, moral traditions are divined from centuries of legislation and other official acts, and the evidence of intended constitutional meaning is manifested in records of complex public debates. Surely, all those words cannot be plainer than the words in the document itself.

Mainstream legal thinking answers all these difficulties with some version of the word "principle." The general words in the Constitution are said to represent principles, just as all the other layers of words in multiple authoritative sources convey principles. Principles constrain judges because they are the moral purposes inherent in the words themselves. They come from the legal materials, not the justice. Thus Kennedy told Senator Grassley that the concept of human dignity in the due process clause must fit with the "purpose of the Constitution." Or consider John Roberts' confident answer to the question with which Senator Biden had bedeviled Justice Rehnquist. Roberts said that the equal protection clause can be used to prevent discrimination against women because it was purposefully written in general language to convey a principle broad enough to apply to gender discrimination.

It remains true, however, that despite the discipline provided by discerning principles in multiple kinds of legal materials, the dominant modern view is that the judge's personality and values will still play a part in interpretation. But, as nominee O'Connor emphasized, the personal is further constrained by conventional legal processes. She said, "I do feel that a judge is constrained by the processes surrounding the judicial system to resolving issues based on the framework of the particular case that has come before the judge, the particular facts, ... and the law applicable to those." Other nominees, notably Ruth Bader Ginsburg, referred to the same idea when they emphasized that judges can only respond to the case that is brought to them and are under an obligation to decide each case on suitably narrow grounds. Virtually all the nominees emphasized professional training and personal integrity. Justices, one nominee after another have said, should try to be restrained, should attempt to avoid legislating, and should strive to be true to the legal materials before them. The sophisticated view, then, is that an understanding of the nature of a legal principle, coupled with professional structures and norms, can prevent justices from an unrestrained pursuit of their own notions of progress. The Constitution may change or be kept up to date or even live, but it will still be the same Constitution.

There are many jurisprudential and practical questions that can be raised about this modern consensus on law and judging. In the next two chapters I ask a different kind of question: Whether or not the way modern lawyers understand interpretation is sound as a matter of theory, what does thinking this way do to a person? What are the psychological implications for modern judges?

5

Realistic Legalism

The preceding chapter describes the way that modern lawyers do and do not understand constitutional interpretation as that understanding emerges from the testimony of Supreme Court nominees over almost four decades. A central component of the modern approach is the combination of a realistic recognition that judges cannot entirely escape their own personal values with a legalistic demand that they should utilize conventional authoritative sources, such as precedent, text, and history. The conventional sources are thought to provide, not concrete meanings, but general principles that the judge must try to define under current circumstances. Although personal philosophy will inevitably influence the judge's definition of constitutional principle, that influence can be kept within acceptable limits by conscientious effort as well as various professional norms and structures.

Although this understanding of law could not fully emerge until the legal realists completed their theoretical work in the first half of the twentieth century, the combination of realism with legalism has deep roots in American thought. Realism is consistent with the country's pragmatic, no-nonsense traditions. Legalism is consistent with an equally deep-seated fascination with law and commitment to the rule of law. It is no surprise, then, that the most influential contemporary legal philosopher, Ronald Dworkin, has spent a career exploring and defending an intellectually elaborate version of what I am calling realistic legalism. And it is no surprise that nearly every law professor in nearly every constitutional law class across the land starts the course with a case that bountifully illustrates realistic legalism, *Marbury v. Madison,* or that *Marbury* has come to have iconic status as the source of the modern practice of judicial review. When Senator Arlen Specter discovered that Robert Bork had serious misgivings about the logic used in *Marbury*, he decided that Bork was outside the mainstream and unfit for the Supreme Court.

Marbury: **The Modern Symbol of Realistic Legalism**

The reason that *Marbury* has taken on such iconic status as the basis for judicial authority is that, while it embodies the fundamental problem that politics and law are not entirely separate, it also holds out the promise that they can be successfully combined. Chief Justice Marshall was a Federalist eager to assert judicial control over Jeffersonians, who occupied the executive department. (Since the case involved his own behavior in the past administration in failing to deliver the judicial commissions at issue, he may even have been interested in depicting his own mistake as insignificant.) At a more elevated level, Marshall may have been influenced to deny relief to the frustrated justice of the peace by a desire to avoid a confrontation with the political branches. Asserting the power to hold federal statutes unconstitutional, when the statute at issue was what gave the Court authority to hear the case, was a way to achieve all of this.

But most commentators agree that asserting the power to set aside statutes as unconstitutional was probably the best—but certainly not the only possible—interpretation of the Constitution. The interpretation of the Court's constitutional powers in *Marbury* was, in short, persuasive but not at all the only possible reading of the Constitution. It could have been a consequence of conscientious attention to conventional legal materials, such as constitutional text and the overall purpose of the document, but it also could have been a consequence of personal and partisan considerations. That *Marbury* can be seen simultaneously as legal statesmanship and raw politics helps to account for our fascination with the case and for its exalted status in our modern political culture.

There is, however, a competing view of *Marbury*. This dissenting view insists that *Marbury* represents, not so much a mixture of legalism and politics as a prototypical and admirable effort to decide a constitutional case on the basis of law. This idea is deserving of careful evaluation because it is influential within certain conservative intellectual circles, including those that have helped to shape the thinking of Scalia, Thomas, Roberts, and Alito. Thus, the dissenting understanding of *Marbury* raises the possibility that what I am calling realistic legalism—as widespread as it is—may not now be, and certainly is not destined to be, the dominant approach to interpretation on the Court.

The legalistic defense of *Marbury* began in earnest in 1986 with the appearance of Christopher Wolfe's important book, *The Rise of Modern Judicial Review*. For Wolfe, *Marbury* is not the primary source of modern judicial review. For one thing, that case was not a self-contained intellectual effort; it reflected widespread understandings about the nature of the judicial function and of constitutionalism as expressed in other cases and in non-judicial sources like *Federalist* No. 78. For another, modern judicial review is a starkly different enterprise from what was authorized by *Marbury*. According to Wolfe, the former consists in self-conscious acts of judicial creativity ("will") while the latter, as practiced by Chief Justice Marshall, consisted in good-faith, conscientious efforts to interpret the Constitution as a legal document ("judgment"). Consequently, the sources of modern judicial review must be sought in historical and intellectual trends quite extrinsic (and even antithetical) to *Marbury*. Thus Wolfe suggests that the judicial function gradually changed because of a natural urge among judges to amass power and to express their idealism, because of a widening gulf between the values common in the legal profession and those common in the general population, and because of the triumph of a realistic modern legal philosophy.

Although Wolfe's distinction between traditional and modern forms of judicial review may sound naïve to some, it is not. Indeed, his account of Justice Marshall's understanding of the nature of legal interpretation is thoughtful and nuanced. It is neither literalistic nor woodenly attached to concrete historical intentions. Instead, Wolfe claims that during the traditional period there was widespread agreement that specific words had to be understood in their context, including the purposes and nature of the whole instrument within which they appear. Moreover, he repeatedly acknowledges that agreement about interpretive rules does not assure agreement about interpretive outcomes even on fundamental issues. In Wolfe's view, the value of traditional legal interpretation is not that it produces determinate results but that it "narrow[s] the range of differences … and provides[s] a common standard for deciding issues." In the end, Wolfe's contrast between traditional and modern interpretation has as much to do with attitude and effort as with constraint and determinacy. The traditional judge intended in good faith to interpret the document and believed this to be possible. The modern judge intends to "legislate" (to impose his or her own preferences) rather than to find the meaning of the document.

Wolfe acknowledges, however, that this difference does not mean that the traditional judge's view of constitutional meaning was wholly independent of his political preferences. Judgments about the political theory embedded in the Constitution could, for instance reflect *both* the personal philosophy of a traditional judge and actual constitutional principles. The traditional judge might, then, sometimes give effect to his own views but (at least ideally) only when they coincided with correct constitutional meaning.

When personal preferences were confounded with abstract constitutional meaning, how certain could a traditional judge be about having accurately identified that meaning? Wolfe's phrasing is careful. He says that that "strong" arguments could be made about the correct content of constitutional principles and that knowledge of such principles was a "valuable aid" in interpretation. In short, for the traditional judge law and politics were not entirely separate, but accurate constitutional interpretation was nevertheless possible because some legal arguments, while not altogether conclusive, were simply stronger than others. Thus, despite the sharp rhetorical divide that he draws between the modern practice of judicial legislation and the traditional practice of objective interpretation, Wolfe in fact provides an account of traditional judging that in significant measure is compatible with realistic accounts.

Therefore, when Wolfe turns to rehabilitating *Marbury v. Madison*, his claims are modest and in many ways not inconsistent with realistic legalism. For example, on the charge that Marshall should have removed himself from the case because he had been personally involved in the relevant events, Wolfe suggests that Marshall was not always concerned with conventional expectations. This, of course, is more a description than a defense, and Wolfe adds to it only some mild speculations about possible high-minded motivations that might, in fact, be fairly described as involving political as much as legal considerations.

On Marshall's interpretation of the federal statute that provided jurisdiction to the Court, Wolfe provides a textual defense for Marshall's somewhat surprising conclusion that the statute authorized the case to be brought directly to the Supreme Court without prior proceedings in a lower court. But he does not deny that the wording of the statute would allow the opposite conclusion. Indeed, Wolfe does not even deny that Marshall might have been motivated to construe the jurisdictional statute as he did because this would allow him to establish the power of judicial review in a politically palatable circumstance. Wolfe actually goes on to describe the political setting and simply characterizes Marshall's motivations in that setting as high-mindedly institutional (or, in Wolfe's term "constitutional") rather than partisan. But Wolfe's own analysis demonstrates that these high-minded purposes, such as avoiding presidential non-enforcement of the Court's order, cannot be entirely separated from partisan purposes, since the order would have issued from a judiciary controlled by partisan Federalists and would have been resisted by a highly partisan Republican president. To say that an opinion "simply denying jurisdiction" would have "detracted from the public position of a judicial branch that had not yet thoroughly established its respectability or power…", is, as Wolfe comes close to acknowledging, to supplement rather than to deny the charges of institutional self-aggrandizement and partisanship.

On the issue of judicial review itself Wolfe's analysis is also surprisingly consistent with realistic legalism. Wolfe does argue that a power of judicial review is "the most reasonable interpretation of the Constitution," but he does not think that any of the arguments against it can be "dismissed as wrong." In fact, Wolfe sounds like a realistic legalist when he writes:

> There is no necessary problem with judges giving effect to unconstitutional laws, any more than with presidents enforcing unconstitutional laws passed over their vetos. In both cases they are not responsible for the unconstitutionality per se—the blame for that belongs to the legislature. One can easily imagine a polity in which judges and executives were not permitted to consider whether laws violated the Constitution, but simply took the laws as they were given, and enforced them.

Judicial review, then, is not a necessary logical inference from the nature of a written constitution. Indeed, for Wolfe it is the best interpretation of our Constitution only if the practice is strictly limited in ways that are consistent with the larger institutional principles that animate his argument.

It is, as I have noted, entirely consistent with realistic legalism to believe that some limited form of judicial review is the best interpretation of the Constitution, at least if the arguments advanced in *Marbury* are supplemented by arguments about the theory that underlies our form of government. It is, on the other hand, entirely consistent with Wolfe's legalistic defense of the decision to believe that this interpretation is debatable rather than inevitable. And it seems to me to be consistent with both positions to believe that the members of Marshall's Court thought that conscientious legal interpretation was possible and that they were engaged in it. And, finally, this last belief is not incompatible with acknowledging that personal and partisan considerations may have had a part to play in how those justices conceived and evaluated the complicated issues before them.

In short, while Wolfe presents his account of *Marbury* as an alternative to the dominant modern view, his position is in fact a version of that view.[1] To the extent that nominees like Roberts and Alito have been influenced by Wolfe's writings or those of other similar conservative thinkers, they are within the mainstream of realistic legalism.

Legalistic Realism in the Work of the Court

If it is a requirement for elevation to the Court that nominees exhibit satisfactory commitment to realistic legalism, we should certainly expect to see the influence of that approach demonstrated in the Court's work product. But is it even possible to implement a legal philosophy that to a large degree combines opposites? One way to answer this question is to imagine what the Court's record would look like if the justices did not combine these approaches.

If the Court were dominated by realists, the results are easy to imagine. If justices believed that it was wholly appropriate to implement their personal or political values, they would not refer to conventional legal authorities at all. They might offer no explanations for their decisions (since all that matters is the outcome). Or they might feel obliged to state what personal beliefs the decision is designed to achieve and maybe even explain how the decreed result in the case will implement the justices' preferences. Needless to say, decisions are not written in this way. They are loaded with references to conventional legal authorities, including lengthy discussions of precedents and arguments about the intended meaning of the text. It might be said these legalistic components are just window dressing inserted because thoroughgoing realism would amount to blatant lawlessness in the eyes of the profession and probably of the public. Is it possible that modern justices spend their

---

1.   I do not mean to suggest that Wolfe's views are in all respects consistent with the modern realist approach. Some traditionalists, perhaps including Wolfe, believe that certain clauses are sufficiently specific that conclusive interpretation is possible, while some realists believe that the nature of language is such that some indeterminacy is present even if language is highly specific. The two positions might also differ on the question whether it is ever possible for the human mind to separate its assessment of constitutional considerations from personal or political commitments. Even assuming areas of real disagreement, the accounts have much in common, including the recognition that not all constitutional issues are susceptible to conclusive resolution and that both legal and political considerations are often simultaneously present. In any event, even ideas that can be shown to be ultimately inconsistent can be—and, of course, often are—held at the same time and, thus, may be interacting in the minds of modern judges.

careers intentionally implementing their own values while hiding their realism by appealing to conventional legal authorities that have not in fact influenced their interpretations? Yes, it is possible, but to take this possibility seriously requires a level of disrespect and cynicism that I hope to avoid if possible.

Given the Court's use of conventionally legalistic materials, it might seem that the justices are not realists at all. In fact, one prominent legal scholar, Larry Kramer, claims that the work of the Rehnquist Court is evidence of "legal fundamentalism." In particular, he points to the recent tendency (noted back in Chapter 2) to see constitutional interpretation as being an exclusively judicial prerogative and thus to see any constitutional interpretation done outside the courts as illegitimate. This observer theorizes that the claim of judicial sovereignty is a consequence of a fundamentalist urge to conceive of the Constitution as ordinary law rather than as mixed questions of law and politics. A pure fundamentalist would be someone who believed that all constitutional issues are entirely legal. To the extent that modern justices approach pure fundamentalism, they would believe that the only institution that can legitimately interpret any part of the Constitution is the judiciary because only judges should resolve ordinary questions of law.

This is an arresting diagnosis. Without question, it is partly true. Moreover, the word "fundamentalism" connotes unthinking conservatism and thus for many academics it dovetails nicely with their general distaste for the Rehnquist Court. As intellectually arresting and politically skillful as it is, the diagnosis of legalistic fundamentalism does not account for many of the characteristics of modern uses of judicial power and it does not even provide a full explanation for judicial sovereignty.

Consider again one of the most widely noted aspects of modern constitutional interpretation, its astonishing range. The modern Court not only sees most constitutional issues as legal; it also sees most social issues as constitutional. Is this evidence of thoroughgoing legalism? Even if all constitutional issues were entirely legal, it would be quite possible for most political or policy disputes to lie outside the ambit of constitutional law. Moreover, a legal fundamentalist might well be inclined to believe that legalism is an inadequate or dangerous way to resolve the complicated social issues that do lie outside those boundaries. One might have expected, therefore, that, despite their constitutional fundamentalism, at least some justices—and perhaps all of them—would be attempting to interpret the document to apply only to those issues that its terms require and, then, only with that degree of detail that can be compellingly justified.

So, to account for modern practices, we must believe that a working majority of the justices believes that the terms of the Constitution apply to almost all issues of public policy—are convinced, that is, that ordinary legalistic methods must be used to resolve virtually all social issues. Such a belief is possible, of course, and may in fact be widespread, but it would seem inconsistent with the degree of institutional hubris that accompanies the Court's inclination to treat a wide range of issues as constitutional issues. Indeed, unless the justices not only believed that ordinary legal methods must be used to resolve constitutional questions but also harbored the unlikely belief that those methods constitute a superior way to decide almost any moral or political question, they presumably would perform their tasks reluctantly, perhaps even sorrowfully. Reluctant fundamentalist justices would understand and even share public frustration over judicial resolution of policy issues. They would not, therefore, be likely to display the visceral and intense disapproval of non-judicial efforts at interpretation that is common today. Indeed, while fundamentalists might feel it their duty to monopolize constitutional determinations, at least some might sympathize with and respect those in the political arena who tried to influence the Court's decisions.

Finally, "fundamentalism" should have produced a prosaic, if stiff, view of the Court's methods and role. After all, the reason a fundamentalist does not think that people in the political arena have any business doing constitutional interpretation is because that task is thought to involve ordinary legal issues. Why, then, does the modern Court utilize so many nontraditional forms of analysis? What accounts for the pervasiveness of instrumental calculation, interest balancing, and reliance on social science? Why has the fundamentalism that has supposedly gripped the modern Court led to very few unequivocal principles and to no absolutes at all? And why are justices who see constitutional interpretation as a form of ordinary legal work so drawn to grand conceptualizations of the role of the Court? How has fundamentalism led to the idea that it is the Court's business to discover the fundamental principles inherent in our political traditions, or to protect minority interests, or to prevent social disintegration?

The Court's modern record does, of course, have intensely legalistic aspects, but to understand contemporary judicial practices it is necessary to imagine the mind and the psychology of a person who is able to be simultaneously a legalist and a realist. That is, it is necessary to imagine what it means for a person to conceive of law and politics as different but not separable and to believe that an interpretation can be right while not conclusive. A mind that is capable of this combination of beliefs, I submit, is not some bizarre concoction but is a fairly accurate depiction of the way justices in the modern era approach constitutional interpretation. Indeed, it is the dominant American view of constitutional interpretation, the essentials of which have been rehearsed by all of those conservative or moderate nominees to the Court ever since the end of the era of Earl Warren.

Most jurists today do not believe that in interpreting the Constitution they are simply imposing their own personal or political agenda. Unless their long and arduous explanations are set aside as entirely dishonest, justices believe that they are offering the best interpretations of the Constitution based on rigorous interpretive criteria. But, unless they are assumed to be ignorant of basic modern jurisprudence, they also suspect that it is impossible to formulate or apply these criteria independently of individual character or political philosophy. Constitutional law, that is, is thought to subsume the political but also to transcend it.

Paradoxically, it is because constitutional interpretation is viewed as partly but inevitably political, that the modern judicial mind resists the conclusion that many issues are not appropriate for resolution in the courts. That conclusion must be resisted because if the presence of a practical or political component were to disqualify the judiciary, it would seem to follow that all constitutional issues are out of bounds. Moreover, as constitutional decisions accumulate, judges, of course, become more and more accustomed to resolving issues that might have once seemed political, and thus the sense that the Constitution covers only a finite range of issues further recedes, and so does any sense of regret for being under the obligation to decide complex legislative or executive matters. The modern judge not only is accustomed to making such decisions but also knows that, since legal and practical criteria are inseparable, many of the same intellectual resources available in the political arena are also available to the judge. After all, judges down through the ages have been doing law, and in the process they must have also been doing some legislating too. The realistic side of the modern judge's mind unapologetically extracts these policymaking strands and uses them overtly and with increasing confidence. Motivations behind political movements are forthrightly characterized, empirical data is assessed, and the instrumental efficacy of various measures is evaluated.

Modern judges, however, do not simply appropriate these realistic methods; they recast them to suit judicial tastes and habits and institutional requirements. (Politics and law, remember, are inevitably mixed.) Thus, for example, political motivation is treated, not as an exceedingly complex empirical matter, but as a deductive proposition likely to yield the sort of singular conclusion that can justify a case outcome. For example, when the Court said that an anti-gay rights provision enacted by the people of Colorado could only have been the result of animus against homosexuals, the justices took no notice at all of the arguments used to gain enactment. Instead, they inferred the actual motivations of thousands of voters from the broad terms of the law.

Similarly, empirical data that comes in highly systematic form with expert credentials is favored over the messier kinds of data that arise out of human experience and interaction. And instrumental efficacy is assessed on the possibly conclusive basis of objectives that pre-existed the policy rather than on the experimental and never-final basis of objectives discovered during policy implementation. These refinements, being congenial to the relatively cerebral judge, only incline the justices to develop less respect for the rough and tumble of political decision making even as they increasingly invade that territory. As the range of constitutional issues widens, judges become more self-assured and see less reason to share interpretive authority.

This dismissiveness grows into outright intolerance because, even as modern judges are increasingly convinced that courts can resolve practical problems, they are also convinced that there is a distinctly legal component to constitutional issues and they know that they have special expertise on that aspect. The formalistic frame of mind associated with this legal side imparts much besides a sense of expertise and entitlement. While the realist side of the modern judge's mind knows that the Court is deciding highly significant and controversial matters of morality, the formalistic side reassuringly recasts the issue into the manageable form of a single case, and one that must be decided at that. A duty to decide even a single case of great political significance, of course, might itself be daunting but the Court's policymaking methodology (folded into complex legalistic doctrines) provides powerful reassurance. This is partly because decisions, while final and authoritative in themselves, leave room for variation in the future. If the data changes or if a more rational statutory strategy is utilized or if one of the interests in the balance should change, it is open to the Court to permit the political branches to pursue their preferred policies.

Even if controversial decisions seem reassuringly limited, modern judges know that a particular interpretation is not inevitable. This might be expected to generate some pressure for modesty, but modern judges also know that such decisions are good faith attempts to arrive at the best available interpretation. Thus modern judging is characterized by a sense of deep vulnerability (no interpretation can be conclusive) that coexists with a sense of great conviction (this is the best interpretation). Judges know that they cannot in the end overcome disagreement at the same moment that they know their interpretation to be the best one possible. Disagreement, under these circumstances, is a source of profound frustration and anger.

As the judiciary progressively displaces legislative and executive authority and, in the process, incorporates policymaking methods into its own decision making, the fundamentalist claim that only courts can be trusted with ordinary legal issues becomes less and less plausible as a justification for the judiciary's role. Moreover, even as they incorporate the methods of political decision makers, judges exhibit increasing intolerance and even arrogance towards political disagreement. Accordingly, the courts must develop new and grander ways to distinguish themselves from political institutions. Or, to put it another way, the purpose of ordinary law must be elevated. It may be, for instance, that in enforcing text-based rules the Court is also protecting abstract principles of democratic theory. Or, it may be that in the process of resolving cases the Court is also teaching fundamental constitutional values or even preventing political disintegration. In any event, as the conceptualization of the Court's role gets fancier, perceived threats to its authority seem not merely frustrating or even infuriating, but dangerous. The modern drive for judicial monopolization, then, derives not from legal fundamentalism but from an inflated sense of institutional mission. And that sense of mission grew gradually from the interaction between legalism and realism.

The mind of the sophisticated American lawyer seamlessly combines legalism and political realism, as does our society's dominant view of law and of judging. The elements within this combination interact in such a way as to make it difficult to confine the reach of Constitutional law, or to recognize as respectable any decision making method different from that used by the judiciary, or, ultimately, to tolerate contention over the meaning of the Constitution. As we shall see next, certain professional norms and the good intentions of the justices are supposed to hold these powerful impulses in check.

6

High Principle and Self-Restraint

Perhaps the most common theme in the confirmation hearings held after 1969 is that a justice of the Supreme Court should make an effort to avoid overreaching. It is important, so say the nominees, for judges to be aware that their personal experiences and beliefs will influence their decisions and to guard against excessively personalized legal interpretations. Self-knowledge and self-discipline are the keys to staying within the judicial role. At the same time, however, it is also usually agreed that constitutional principles are general because the language that mandates them is general. Ronald Dworkin actually takes this so far as to assert that principles should be conceived at their most general level of abstraction. The attraction of generality is the attraction of moralism. The more general the principle, the more ambitious its moral content. Dworkin and many others have claimed that Robert Bork's view of the Constitution is not true to the document's moral grandeur because Bork thinks that lesser levels of generality are sometimes appropriate.

If we are to understand the mind and the psychology of the modern judge, then, we have to imagine more than the consequences of blending realism and legalism. We also have to imagine the consequences of striving for high principle and self-restraint simultaneously. A useful way to start is to examine a book that struggles mightily with the tension between principle and restraint and that did much to shape the self-image of the modern judge. The book, published in 1962 during the heady days of the Warren Court, is oddly titled *The Least Dangerous Branch*, and the author was an eminent professor of constitutional law at the Yale Law School named Alexander Bickel.

High Principle as Moralism

Bickel's book is famous in part as an argument in favor of what he called "the passive virtues." These are various technical devices that enable the Court to avoid deciding controversial issues. Bickel's argument

77

was that in deciding whether to invoke one of these devices, the Supreme Court could properly consider whether the public would be receptive to its decision if it were to go ahead and decide the case. Much of the early reaction to Bickel's proposal centered on his audacious argument that the justices could properly take into account such overtly political considerations.

Perhaps because the passive virtues enabled the Court to avoid making contentious decisions, less noticed was Bickel's ambitious moralism. But the purpose of judicial passivity was delay and the purpose of delay was to avoid legitimating (and thus entrenching) immoral political practices. The historical model was Lincoln's support for the Missouri Compromise. Bickel noted that because of prudential political considerations Lincoln could not support the immediate abolition of slavery; these considerations, however, did not induce Lincoln to abandon principle and concede the morality of the "evil institution." On the contrary, by opposing the spread of slavery into the territories, Lincoln could remain true to the principle that chattel slavery is incompatible with free government. The realization of the goal of abolition—which as a principle "made sense only as an absolute"—remained for the future, but the goal, the principle, could be asserted in the present. What Bickel called the "educational" value of enunciated principle could influence political events and hasten the day of liberation.

Bickel's idea that imprudent haste can undermine the integrity of moral principle and thus obstruct political progress has as its central juridical model what he termed *Plessy v. Ferguson's* Error. *Plessy*, decided in 1896, is the case that upheld the doctrine of separate but equal. I will have something to say about it in Chapter 7. But the error that Bickel saw in the case was this: Because the Court in *Plessy* did not avoid the question of the constitutionality of segregation, it undermined the principle of equal protection and helped to entrench Jim Crow. In contrast, Bickel provided a veritable pantheon of progressive political goals that he claimed were or might have been advanced by avoidance and delay: the elimination of aid to parochial schools, the desegregation of public schools, the reduction of censorship, the right to use birth control devices, the protection of membership in the Communist Party, the right to equal voting representation, and the elimination of the death penalty.

In itemizing these political goals, I am certainly not suggesting that Bickel's objective was merely ideological. He clearly thought that delay and avoidance served other important kinds of purposes, including responsible democratic decision making and full deliberation about the content of principles. But neither these concerns about process nor Bickel's later explicit embrace of Burkean conservativism should obscure the fact that one of the fundamental impulses behind *The Least Dangerous Branch* was a moralistic urge to achieve reform.

It is a testament to the complexity and richness of Bickel's mind that by 1975, when the Court's wild ride was fully underway, he had come to condemn the very kind of moral idealism that animated *The Least Dangerous Branch*.[1] Writing about the war in Vietnam in *The Morality of Consent*, Bickel commented, "What propelled us into this war was a corruption of the ... idealistic, liberal impulse...." He went on, "[T]he altruistic impulse decayed into self-assurance and self-righteousness...." Rejecting the notion that this deterioration of the liberal's "generous ideology" was caused by individuals' excesses, Bickel concluded:

> [T]he seeds of decay are within the ideologies themselves, in their pretensions to universality, in their over-confident assaults on the variety and unruliness of the human condition, in the intellectual and emotional imperialism of concepts like freedom, equality, even peace.

Reacting not only to the cruelty of the military action in Vietnam, but also to the arrogance and lawlessness of Watergate, Bickel observed that the legal order "cannot sustain the continuous assault of moral imperatives...." He charged that this assault had been mounted not only from "the outside" but from "within," from "the Supreme Court headed for fifteen years by Earl Warren."

If Bickel was right in 1975 about the seeds of decay inherent in ideology itself, it would be peculiar if his earlier prescriptions for the Supreme Court's role—so clearly animated by his own altruistic ideology—somehow should show no evidence of potentially authoritarian self-righteousness. These implications do show up, mainly in the inflated significance that Bickel attributed to the concept of constitutional principle and to the justices who enunciate them. When the Supreme Court announces a principle, Bickel claimed it is doing something that democracy cannot do for itself; it is "inject[ing] into representative government something that is not already there...." Moreover, what would otherwise be missing from democratic government is essential, for "[n]o good society can be

---

1.   Bickel's thinking evolved gradually. Of particular relevance is *The Supreme Court and the Idea of Progress* (1970), where Bickel began to doubt the political practicability of high principle. He suggested that with respect to complex problems, perhaps "society is best allowed to develop its own strands out of its tradition; it moves forward most effectively ... in empirical fashion (175)."

unprincipled." While the Supreme Court should assert grand principles only sparingly, those principles that are finally announced must be enforced "without adjustment or concession and without let-up." And how do, in Bickel's evocative words, "nine lawyers ... derive principles which they are prepared to impose without recourse upon ... society"? Not merely by consulting conventional legal sources such as constitutional text or history or precedent. No, justices must find "fundamental presuppositions rooted in history to which widespread acceptance may fairly be attributed." To achieve such insight, the nine lawyers must "immerse themselves in the tradition of our society and of kindred societies that have gone before, in history ... and ... in the thought and the vision of the philosophers and the poets." They will then be "fit to extract 'fundamental presuppositions' from their deepest selves...." The ambitiousness and seriousness of this process of derivation justify the dominion of the constitutional principles that emerge.

Just as Bickel conceived of the Court's principles as politically essential, deeply moral, and uncompromisingly authoritative, he depicted them as being in opposition not only to relatively unimportant considerations ("expediency") but also to weak, sometimes dangerous impulses. Thus principles stand in the way of legislative irrationality, which "... only takes a legislature more than normally whipped up, ... acting under severe pressure, rushed, tired, lazy, mistaken, or, forsooth, ignorant." The contrast is between "rationality and uncontrolled emotion...." The Court should impose a "test of a calm judgment resting on allowable inferences drawn from common human experience." How should a justice decide what inferences are "allowable"? What is constitutional, said Bickel, is what "rests on an unquestioned, shared choice of values...."

Contrast this exalted conception of constitutional principle with the more conventional and legalistic conception that it partly displaced. To take the version discussed in *The Least Dangerous Branch*, Bickel's older colleague, Herbert Wechsler, thought of principle as a minimal criterion, as a basic intellectual test meant to assure, not goodness in the society, but minimal integrity in judicial reason giving. Indeed, remember that Wechsler's austere understanding of principle stood as a challenge to the moralism of the school desegregation decision, *Brown v. Board of Education*. In contrast, Bickel extracted the moralism from his conventional reformist ideology and poured it into the idea of principle. For him, principles "derive their worth from a long view of society's spiritual as well as material needs...."

From this position, it was a short but necessary step to elevate the avatars of principle—those nine lawyers—to a superior moral status. This Bickel accomplished in part by idealizing the institutional context of adjudication. Cases, he said, present problems in a concrete setting and well after the agitation surrounding the initial political decision has subsided. Thus "insulation and the marvelous mystery of time give courts the capacity to appeal to men's better natures...." Bickel also relied on a skillful melding of assertion and prescription to make a rather surprising claim: "Judges have, or should have, the leisure, the training, and the insulation to follow the ways of the scholar in pursuing the ends of government." Presumably equipped with a "habit of mind" not unlike that which Bickel himself enjoyed, judges have the skills "crucial in sorting out the enduring values of a society...."

The Bickel of 1975 might well have asked the Bickel of 1962 how the justices—assigned the task of identifying society's enduring and unquestioned values, and urged to believe they enjoyed an almost unique capacity to do so, and instructed to enforce these principles "without concession or let-up"—could avoid "intellectual and emotional imperialism." Indeed, if Bickel had lived into the twenty-first century, he might well have wondered whether *The Least Dangerous Branch* had contributed to four decades of moral imperialism on the part of the federal judiciary.

Self-Restraint and Legal Craft

To imagine this kind of self-criticism no doubt seems unfair, since it ignores the fact that Bickel's appreciation for restraint, or prudence as he called it, was a central aspect of his thinking from the beginning. The richly ambivalent, sometimes tortured intellectualizations about judicial review that make up *The Least Dangerous Branch* represent a protracted struggle between *two* impulses: on the one hand, the dangerous implications of Bickel's moral self-assurance but, on the other, his recognition of the need for prudence. These are precisely the same conflicting impulses that show up so consistently in the testimony of judicial nominees during the modern era. Bickel's argument in *The Least Dangerous Branch*—an argument echoed years later in the testimony of Sandra Day O'Connor and Ruth Bader Ginsburg—was that it is possible for the Court to pursue high moral purposes safely if the justices are hedged in by practices and understandings that assure prudence.

This answer misunderstands the nature of prudence. That set of instincts is not a bulwark against ideological moralism. Prudence is the opposite of ideological moralism. It is what the decay inherent in liberal idealism consumes.

Bickel argued that the Supreme Court can safely be trusted with a role saturated by moralism because deep legalistic norms and practices assure humility, discretion, and restraint. The first of these was the "clear mistake" rule under which judges do not declare a statute unconstitutional unless the judgment of unconstitutionality is "not open to rational question." The second was Wechsler's requirement of neutrality, by which a court's determination must rest on a constitutional consideration "greater than any single concern of the moment." And, of course, Bickel's own contribution was to describe at length how an array of avoidance devices allows justices to insist on the realization of principle only rarely and only when the times are propitious.

Bickel argued that these norms and practices would restrain morally imperious judges from acting too often. He seemed to think they would cause judges to *be* prudent individuals. Thus, in dictating that judges defer to the reasonable judgments of other officials, the clear mistake rule entails patience and caution and tolerance. Decisions must be made slowly and carefully. Fine distinctions, as, for example, between "arbitrary guesses and calculations of probability" must be made. The viewpoints of others must be considered imaginatively and respectfully. All this means that the judge will be inclined to appreciate the full complexity of public issues, to consult all of human experience, and to intervene only with reluctance.

Similarly, to render a decision that transcends the interests of the moment, a judge must be disinterested both politically and psychologically. The testing of reasons and the striving for intellectual coherence that are inherently a part of neutrality necessitate rigor and self-discipline. And because neutral principles must be enforced uniformly—without "adjustment or concession"—they are intrinsically sobering. Plainly, their announcement involves considerable risk and, so, it should be obvious that "there can be but very few such principles."

Because their purpose is delay, the avoidance devices that Bickel described as such a pervasive part of the record of the Supreme Court require, needless to say, self-control. They also require attention to the widest array of social and cultural factors, including most especially attention to the opinions of others, because one purpose of delay is to impose principles at a time close to when society is ready to accept them. Moreover, delay allows events and consequences to take form so that the content of principle can be shaped by experience. Indeed, Bickel went so far as to argue that this experience includes the opinions and objections that develop in response to principles that the Court has already enunciated and imposed. Humbled by all this unruly information, then, the justices will not be authoritarian moralists; they will be teachers of society, learning as well as speaking, engaged in nothing more dangerous than a continuing "colloquy."

In short, while Bickel freely blended description and prescription, the strongest version of his argument is that norms embedded in their task require, and thus will gradually instill, capacities for caution, self-restraint, circumspection, and humility. His argument, then, is not merely an exhortation to the justices that in order to resist the dangers inherent in a profoundly moralistic role they *should* carry out their responsibilities in a prudent way. His argument is a claim that, at least if institutional norms are understood and respected, the Court *can* be trusted with the "grand function" of protecting principle because its members will tend to develop an adequate capacity for prudence. The prudent character of the justices will domesticate the moralistic nature of constitutional principle. That is why the most powerful court on earth is also the least dangerous branch.

The Futility of Prudent Moralism

The great difficulty with this subtle and powerful position is that prudent individuals would not want to exercise, indeed, would not be capable of exercising, the role that Bickel assigned to the Supreme Court. Prudence is not a bulwark against that kind of power; prudence is its repudiation. Or, to turn the matter around, a judge who assigned principle the high meaning and purpose that Bickel urged would not be a prudent person. A judge imprudent enough to try to impose enduring, universal values would act imprudently even while utilizing the various devices intended to domesticate principle. This is to say that the principled reformer, in contrast to the capacious scholar who civilizes moralism through wide and respectful colloquy, to a considerable degree is uneducable.

Consider Bickel's claim that in holding out and enforcing timeless principles, the Supreme Court is providing the democratic process something that it cannot provide for itself. This assertion is plainly untrue, as Bickel's own account of Abraham Lincoln's position on the Missouri Compromise demonstrates. Even without this striking instance, on what basis would anyone believe that politics is somehow incompatible with the articulation of enduring values? If such values are timeless, they must have long been recognized to be so—and not primarily by federal judges. Indeed, this is implicit in the judicial methodology that Bickel himself proposed, inasmuch as he claimed that the justices' task is to steep themselves in the work of the great thinkers and in society's shared, unquestioned choice of values. And since Bickel claimed that these values are truly fundamental to both national identity and political morality, their importance presumably could be apparent even to ordinary people and political arguments on their behalf at least sometimes widely persuasive.

It is difficult to account for Bickel's improbable insistence that only the Court can be depended upon to articulate and enforce enduring principles except as an instance of the authoritarian dynamic inherent in abstract idealism. If principles are primarily intellectualizations, it is natural to devalue or even shut out voices that speak concretely or experientially. And Bickel did write as if the common vocabulary of politics—the language of self-interest and emotion and pragmatism—were irrelevant to understanding or formulating the great goals of a polity. What is clear about Bickel's sharp demarcation between principle and politics, then, is that it drastically restricts the kinds of colloquy thought to be appropriate.

This restriction, however, is only the beginning of the principled reformer's imperviousness. Because principles are virtuous ideals, dissenting intellectualizations (while technically relevant) will naturally be suspect and, indeed, only a short step from representing obduracy or evil. Moreover, because principles are universal, those who argue for exceptions and qualifications will be seen as compromisers and carpers. Because principles are conceptualizations, empirical information about practicalities and costs will be resisted. In fact, because principles are timeless, there will be a tendency to classify all competing information as temporary or short-run or otherwise unimportant.

As I have already indicated, copious signs of all this can be found throughout *The Least Dangerous Branch*. Remember, from strenuous effort ("immersion") the justices ascertain "unquestioned" truths. Their minds stand against society's "uncontrolled emotions." True, these judicial moralists are to come to the point of action only slowly and then only in rare instances of indefensible irrationality and then only on the basis of considerations that transcend any immediate circumstance. But since the main purpose of delay is to hold reform until the time is ripe, Bickel viewed the factors that require delay as generally regrettable. Certainly, Bickel wanted social conditions and common understandings to be assessed, but mainly for the purpose of discovering when these frustrating impediments (those emotions, that self-interest) have sub-sided to a manageable level. When that moment arrives, he insisted that there is no longer any reason, including any objections that may still be held in the political arena, not to impose principle. It is true that the obligation of colloquy persists after the imposition of principle. But because the constitutional value was arrived at through difficult reflection, is timeless and so clear as to be beyond rational dispute, even intellectualized objections raised after the Court's decree neces-sarily carry a heavy presumption of illegitimacy. For Bickel, after all, the advantage of judicial review was that enduring principles can be consistently held out.

Alexander Bickel helped to make respectable the idea that the func-tion of the Supreme Court is to inject into our political life sufficient appreciation for enduring, essential, unquestionable moral principles. He proposed that this educational role could be fulfilled by imposing the principles without remorse or compromise. He made this imperious role seem safe by insisting that justices imprudent enough to attempt it would nevertheless become prudent in exercising it. This transformation would be accomplished through the benignly cautionary influence of certain poorly understood but deeply rooted judicial norms. The difficulty is that these norms, in the hands of imprudent judges, only spur on the kind of moral imperialism that Bickel was seeking to avoid.

The Consequences of Prudent Moralism

No one can say, of course, whether *The Least Dangerous Branch* is in any measure responsible for the decades of judicial imperialism that followed its publication. It is entirely possible that Bickel and the justices were independently moved by the same great institutional and jurisprudential currents. However, given Bickel's prominence and given how flatteringly seductive his depiction of the judicial role must have been, it is also possible that his book encouraged the justices on their path. What can be said with assurance, I think, is that the general contours of the Court's record have a striking resemblance to what I have argued should be expected if restraining legal norms are consumed by the fires of abstract principle.

Consider again the pervasiveness of constitutional law in the modern era. The promiscuousness of constitutional interpretation is a natural outgrowth of the moral idealism that underlies the modern Court's func-tion. Because the Court's goals—equality, autonomy, liberation, and so on—are thought to represent profound and timeless moral principles, the need for their realization is felt urgently and the opportunity for their realization is perceived everywhere.

The justices, of course, sometimes acknowledge the wisdom of selectivity and caution, and these considerations are occasionally decisive. But this impulse is limited by the justices' inability to see or respect disagreement among the public. Since disagreement is largely unthinkable, for the most part the justices perceive the public as compliant. Even when the issue is undeniably controversial as a moral matter, like abortion or homosexuality, or when it is politically controversial, like presidential confidentiality or selection, they tend to believe their decisions will gain sufficient consent. Given the scale of their mission, the justices see objections that fall short of outright defiance as unimportant and, often, profoundly misguided or even improper. The time, consequently, usually seems propitious.

A second characteristic of the Court's modern record that I have noted is that, despite the moral and institutional hubris that drives the Court's campaigns, for the most part the decisions themselves do not seem highly principled. Lofty goals are often stated but not consistently implemented. Instead, the articulation of goals is accompanied by pages devoted to pragmatic considerations, potential qualifications, and inconclusive doctrines. To some extent, this hesitation and instrumentalism are also a consequence of the exalted educative role that the Court has assumed. Since it is thought to be absolutely crucial that society be made to understand, say, that women must be free to choose their own destinies or that people must be judged as individuals and rather than as members of racial groups, the Court is naturally tempted to make such pronouncements before the time for consistent imposition has arrived. After all, realization can be postponed, but—without immediate articulation of principle by the courts—society will lose sight of essential truths. Thus, when the fact of serious disagreement does register, the justices are inclined to see it as reason to plunge ahead on articulation even while hedging on implementation.

Oddly, when the Court *is* ready to implement its lofty goals, its decisions are still often characterized by narrowness and by protracted utilitarian analysis. This, too, is a consequence of the Court's exalted role. Its intellectual burden, after all, is to demonstrate that nothing justifies the law under review, that the law is unconstitutional beyond any rational dispute. The elaborate consideration of justifications, then, is not so much part of political dialogue as a sustained effort to disparage the political aspirations and judgments that stand in the way of principle.

Think again about that most surprising aspect of constitutional jurisprudence at the end of the twentieth century: despite opposition strong enough to cause presidents and senators to call for judicial "restraint" and to install judicial "conservatives" and "moderates" on the Court, no landmark decision has been reversed and many have been validated and expanded. As we have seen, far from being humbled or restrained by political controversy, the justices have reacted to political agitation by asserting repeatedly that their constitutional interpretations are supreme and that disagreement is illegitimate. Moreover, for substantial periods of time and on significant issues (ranging from school desegregation to abortion to school prayer) the Court's reaction to disagreement has been to widen, not constrict, its contested holdings. Like the other prominent characteristics of the Supreme Court's record, this is not what Bickel recommended. But it, too, is a consequence of the exalted sense of purpose that he did endorse.

The modern Court accepts the idea that its role is central to civilized government—that it provides ideals, which are both essential and otherwise unavailable. Maintaining the Court's authority, therefore, is thought to be more important than any justice's particular interpretive commitments. And maintaining that authority is far more important than learning from clamoring political opposition; indeed, the justices are less inclined to listen to or learn from this opposition to the extent that its criticisms are heartfelt and to the extent that the constitutional issue is fundamental. Fervent challenges on fundamentals might make for a good seminar, but they represent a strong threat to the Court's authority.

Since the publication of *The Least Dangerous Branch*, the Supreme Court has been both powerful and dangerous. It has intervened often because pervasive oversight has seemed prudent. It has held out high principles while explaining itself pragmatically. It has taken on an exalted educative function without engaging in respectful dialogue. It has demonstrated that legal norms which might otherwise be expected to produce intellectual discipline and personal restraint become so much fuel when set afire by the idealism of principle.

7

The Mantra of Legal Authority

Despite what I have said in the last two chapters, there remains, I suspect, something irresistible about the idea of a conscientious, self-disciplined judge. Assume for a moment that I am right that the basic elements of modern legal thought—that is, the combination of realism with legalism and of principle with prudence—interact in ways that tend to expand the role of the modern Supreme Court. Nevertheless, it must also seem that that putting judicial moderates or conservatives on the Court will lead to fewer interventions in the nation's political and cultural affairs than would elevating wild-eyed idealists. Surely, there is a difference between Rehnquist and Warren, between Alito and Brennan. And if this is so, it must be true that putting just one more judicial conservative on the Court (so as to make five reliably restrained votes) would cause a major change in course. This is what might be called "the lure of the next nominee."

As common sense suggests, the record since 1970 does demonstrate that the judicial philosophies of nominees do matter, at least to a degree. Neither the Burger Court nor the Rehnquist Court had the same record that a second or third Warren Court would have had. And it is too early to be sure how much difference the appointments of Roberts and Alito will make. But the record so far demonstrates that the changes induced by post-Warren Court appointees do not reduce the potent overall role that the judiciary plays in American politics and culture. The Supreme Court continues to change fundamental constitutional understandings at a fast clip, and it continues to cause unease, conflict, centralization, and estrangement. The question that should concern us is not whether new appointees might tack one way or another but whether they might turn the Supreme Court enough to significantly reduce this cultural damage.

Again, assume that modern history supports my view that the answer to this important question is that as long as successful, sophisticated lawyers are those being nominated, differences in ideology or philosophy will not make much difference to overall direction. Still, there is an aspect of modern legal thinking that would seem to make it possible for the appointment of additional able and restrained justices in the years ahead to eventually turn the Court. After all, the mind of the American lawyer, as I have described it, does understand that traditional sources of legal authority—which lie outside the justices' personality and ideology and philosophy—should be consulted and should help determine how constitutional cases are decided. Indeed, these conventional sources of authority are offered as a kind of mantra at confirmation hearings. In different combinations and with different emphases, nominee after nominee offers them up: text, history, tradition, precedent, and the overall logic of the document.

The Mirage of Personal Restraint

"The lure of the next nominee" rests, I think, on a simple intuition. That intuition is that some people are more inclined or better able than are others to maximize reliance on these external sources of authority and to minimize the influence of the personal. The jurist whom nominees frequently invoke as a model for this kind of restrained, conscientious judge is John Marshall Harlan (actually the second man with this name to serve on the Court). Harlan was, no doubt, a thoughtful and careful judge, and judges like him are part of the lore of legal education. He was, in fact, very much in the model of the learned judicial statesman that Alexander Bickel exalted in *The Least Dangerous Branch*. Like Bickel's idealization, Harlan believed in articulating and protecting principles embedded deep in the traditions of western civilization. He believed in narrow, restrained decisions and in fidelity to precedent and other sources of legal authority. Nevertheless, it is doubtful that he did much to reduce the extent of the Court's power.

His famous and admired opinion in *Cohen v. California* (1971) found it irredeemably dangerous (indeed, antithetical to "the premise of individual dignity and choice upon which our political system rests") to allow a state to prohibit public displays of profanity. This decision became the intellectual fountainhead for dozens of decisions during the modern era that drastically restricted governmental authority to set minimal standards for public discourse. Harlan also wrote a famous dissent arguing for a constitutional right to use contraceptives. In the hands of other justices, this position eventually ripened into the many cases protecting a right to sexual freedom and abortion. Finally, Harlan was responsible for the

Court's insistence ("it should go without saying") that the courts cannot be influenced by political disagreement when enforcing the desegregation principle. From this august understanding of judicially announced principle grew the hysterical claims to judicial sovereignty found in *Planned Parenthood v. Casey.*

How could a deep commitment to the mantra of conventional legal authority fail to prevent the unleashing of so much judicial power in so many directions? Devotion to the mantra does not restrain judges because it merely states that they should refer to a mixed set of sources of legal authority while providing no guidance as to how to weigh the various elements when they conflict with one another. Thus, no amount of conscientious attention to constitutional text or history or precedent will remove the influence of the judge's personal values because those values are what determine whether text or history or precedent should be more important in any particular case. For Harlan, precedent was highly important in the free speech case but not in the contraception case. What was important in the case first asserting judicial sovereignty over constitutional meaning was not history or precedent but the structural logic of the Constitution as a whole.

In short, even as the mantra of legal authority directs our attention to the various forms of legal constraint, it liberates judges to exercise their own choice about outcome. Given the conventions of modern legal interpretation, I doubt that this freedom is avoidable. A jurist as able and as devoted to limits on judicial power as Justice Scalia can be seen making the inevitable choices among different sources of authority. He had to choose between constitutional text and original intent when deciding on the scope of immunity that state governments have against federal judicial power, and he chose original intent. He had to choose between a principled reading of text and original meaning when deciding on the scope of a state's power to engage in affirmative action, and in this instance he chose text. He had to choose between a principled reading of the text and political traditions in deciding whether so-called "fighting words" are exempt from free speech protection, and he chose a principled reading of the text. He had to choose between a principled reading of text and political traditions in deciding whether political patronage violates freedom of speech, and in this instance he chose political traditions.

The freedom to choose among types of legal authority is no minor glitch in the system. Many, if not most, constitutional decisions of the modern era are arguably inconsistent with the intentions of those who framed and ratified the Constitution. Therefore, a choice to follow precedent will often lead to ahistorical interpretations. Since the justices can opt for either precedent or historical meaning, they are often, maybe always, free to choose opposite outcomes. The situation is actually worse than this because, as we have seen, the justices are also free to factor in the other components of the mantra to whatever degree they think appropriate. Thus if precedents differ from both text and history, jurists can still decide to stay with those prior decisions, perhaps throwing in some ruminations about the underlying structure of the whole document.

The practical consequences of this freedom are enormous. Respect for precedent requires not only that the justices normally follow the specific outcomes of prior cases, but also that they follow their logic. The logic of legions of cases demands that judges second-guess legislative and executive decisions on the most sensitive moral and political issues and that judges decide for themselves on the appropriate means for achieving preferred policies. These demands are formalized in elaborate legal doctrines that require, for example, that a restriction on speech be necessary to achieve a compelling governmental interest or that a gender distinction be likely to serve an important public purpose. I will return in the next chapter to the problems created by such doctrines. But the simple fact is that constitutional law as set out in the cases now requires judges, at least when they choose to follow precedent, to legislate from the bench. Nominees to the Court can repeat endlessly that judges should interpret, not make, law. But unless they are willing, once on the Court, to rethink the logic of legions of prior cases, they will be free not only to subordinate text and history but also to make legislative judgments.

Precedent and Authoritarianism

It is not surprising, therefore, that precedent is a frequent subject in modern confirmation hearings. Some nominees refer senators to the various factors that the Supreme Court has from time to time indicated are relevant to deciding when to depart from prior decisions. The truth may have been revealed during the hearings for nominee Scalia, who, despite his strong belief in clear rules that provide for constraint and predictability, told the Judiciary Committee that the value of precedent "can only be answered in the context of a particular case."

With so much riding on a nominee's philosophy about the importance of precedent (or in legalese "*stare decisis*") senators are not always satisfied with answers as vague as Scalia's. At the outset of Samuel Alito's confirmation hearings, the chairman of the Senate Judiciary Committee, Senator Arlen Specter, asked a series of questions on the subject. Eventually the questions took an odd turn with Specter asking Alito whether he agreed that the right to abortion had special immunity from reconsideration, that is, whether it is "super-precedent." Alito parried this by declining to "get into categorizing precedents as super-precedents or super-duper-precedents." That sort of terminology, Alito said, reminded him "of the size of the laundry detergent in the supermarket." This exchange, which must have puzzled most Americans, was highly significant. It presented to the public a version of the Supreme Court's most ambitious effort to define when justices must put precedent above the other factors in the mantra of legal authorities.

Although the practice of sticking with precedent is often associated in popular understanding with stodgy legalism, it was a shrewd subject for Specter to choose in a political setting. Alito, like any good lawyer, makes his living by working from the logic of prior cases. Moreover, a reluctance to disrespect or to unsettle prior understandings is especially natural for someone with conservative instincts. Thus, while it is doubtful that Alito thinks that the Court's abortion decision, *Roe v. Wade*, was solidly based in the Constitution, it is certainly possible that he might be too devoted to precedent to overrule it. Other Republican appointees—including Justices O'Connor, Kennedy, and Souter—refused in *Planned Parenthood v. Casey* to overrule *Roe* largely because they thought it was entitled to a special degree of respect as precedent. If the original abortion decision is super-precedent and the Court in *Casey* emphatically affirmed that extraordinary status, then *Casey* must be super-duper-precedent. So the issue that Senator Specter was raising was whether the justices are required in at least a small class of cases to honor precedent over the other kinds of authority that make up the legal mantra.

There are some cases that as a practical matter are not subject to reconsideration. As Senator Specter has pointed out in various confirmation hearings through the years, the iconic *Marbury v. Madison* is not going to be overruled, nor is the Supreme Court going to consider overruling it. The same is true for the school desegregation decision, *Brown v. Board of Education*. Such precedents are beyond reconsideration, not because they are intellectually unassailable, but because for a variety of reasons they are so widely accepted by the public and the legal profession that it would not occur to any serious lawyer to challenge them.

Used in this way, the idea of a "super-precedent" is superfluous. A judicial decision is beyond direct challenge when it would not occur to anyone to attempt such a challenge. Some of the specific cases that Specter asked Alito about—for example, the decision establishing a constitutional right of minors to contraceptives—are not super-precedents in this sense. And the abortion decisions, which were his main concern, are bitterly contested, as is evident from the enactment of a federal partial birth abortion ban and any number of state statutes that are designed to nibble away at the right to abortion. In defending such laws, very serious lawyers have mounted, and will mount, challenges to the Court's abortion precedents.

Various reasons are offered for staying with a constitutional decision that can be (or has been) challenged. One mentioned by Specter is that people order their affairs in reliance on judicial decisions. There is, obviously, a cost in disturbing settled expectations. However, it is only necessary to notice another of the senator's concerns to see that these costs cannot by themselves always be a decisive factor. In fact, it was just prior to broaching the notion of a super-precedent that Specter asked whether Alito agreed that the Constitution embodies "the concept of a living thing" and that it "represents the values of a changing society." By now it should go without saying that in attempting to keep the Constitution up-to-date, the justices have frequently shattered the established expectations of millions of Americans.

In fact, as we saw in Chapter 3, what no one for over a century and a half had even thought to propose—for instance, that the Constitution protects a right to abortion or prohibits patronage systems—has over and over again been suddenly announced by the Court. These sweeping changes, I say again, sometimes upset laws passed in every state, and they often undermine deeply entrenched moral norms and behaviors. (Consider, as just one possibility, the impact on social practices and widely shared understandings if the Court were to accept the invitation to keep the Constitution changing with the times by declaring heterosexual marriage laws unconstitutional.) A Court that has repeatedly set about transforming society cannot be dedicated to predictability as an overriding value.

It might be objected that it is different for the Court to unsettle expectations that it had no role in creating than for it to unsettle expectations created by its own precedents. However, in important and highly celebrated instances the Court has swept aside practices and understandings that had been validated by the Court's own prior decisions. Go back, for example, to 1896 when in the notorious case of *Plessy v. Ferguson* the Supreme Court determined that racially segregated public facilities did not violate the requirement of equal protection of the laws as long as the facilities were physically equal. In reliance on this decision, states across the south extended Jim Crow until public services ranging from schools to drinking fountains were legally segregated.

This apartheid, as everyone knows, remained legally entrenched until 1954, when the Supreme Court in *Brown* held that racially segregated schools could not be equal. *Brown*, now an acknowledged illustration of an unchallengeable precedent, began the destruction of a way of life that the Court itself had helped to put in place. The cruelty and prejudice inherent in that way of life should not obscure what decades of bitter, sometimes violent resistance to desegregation amply demonstrate—that the Court's long campaign against segregation was an assault on deeply held expectations and long established patterns of behavior. Obviously, some things are more important than public reliance on judicial decisions.

When the Court in *Casey* announced that *Roe* was a kind of super-precedent, it pointed to a range of ways in which people had come to rely on the right to abortion. It distinguished this reliance from the settled social expectations created by *Plessy* on the ground that the doctrine of "separate but equal" had rested on the factual assumption that legal separation of the races did not imply the inferiority of blacks unless (as the infamous *Plessy* Court put it) "the colored race chooses to put that construction upon it." By 1954 "society's understanding of [these] facts" had changed. Thus, explained the Court, the public could see the overruling of *Plessy* as being based on a new understanding of human psychology rather than on a change of legal principle. No such change in factual understandings could, the Court concluded, justify the defeat of the expectations generated by *Roe*.

Our current situation, then, is that the decision to overrule the separate but equal doctrine is the most celebrated legal event of the twentieth century, while the decision establishing a right to abortion, the most legally dubious and controversial opinion of the twentieth century, is an untouchable super-precedent. To say the least, this deserves some reflection.

It is true that *Plessy* contains the factual claims that the Court in *Casey* quoted. And it is also true that *Brown*, relying on some dubious social science, asserts the opposite understanding of the psychology of segregation. The existence of these empirical claims in *Brown*, however, does not justify the Court's insistence that overruling *Roe* would be understood by the public as a more basic revision of legal principle than was overruling the doctrine of separate but equal.

While *Plessy* relied on some psychological speculations, it also stood for the broad principle that the equal protection clause was not intended "to enforce social equality, or a commingling of the two races upon terms unsatisfactory to either." Similarly, while *Brown* relied on some psychological and educational speculations, it also stands for the broad principle that the equal protection clause does prohibit social inequality between blacks and whites. If there was any doubt about this broader meaning in 1954, it was quickly eliminated in the next few years as courts ordered the desegregation of public beaches, buses, golf courses, and bathhouses. In short, the most celebrated decision of our time did overrule an established legal principle upon which pervasive political expectations and moral understandings had been based.

In contrast, the Court could have overruled *Roe* without reversing any constitutional or legal principle. The *Casey* opinion begins by carefully laying out the essential aspects of *Roe* that it was declining to overrule. The first of these was that the Constitution protects the right to abortion and, therefore, "[b]efore viability, the State's interests are not strong enough to support a prohibition of abortion or the imposition of a substantial obstacle to the woman's effective right to elect the procedure." Now, the claim that the Constitution protects a right to abortion is an interpretive legal principle, in kind much like the claim in *Plessy* that the equal protection clause does not require social equality. But the proposition that a state's interests before about the sixth month of pregnancy are not strong enough to justify prohibiting abortions or imposing substantial obstacles on abortions is not a legal principle at all. It is a moral conclusion representing a judgment about the relative importance of what appear to be two entirely incommensurate interests, the individual interest of a woman in obtaining abortions and the moral interest of the state in regulating or prohibiting early-term abortions.

It is an arresting question how a judge can assess whether the wide array of purposes that a woman can have in seeking an abortion are more important than a state's interest in, say, protecting potential human life or keeping a husband appraised of his wife's plan to terminate her pregnancy. And it is an interesting question how such determinations are different in any way from legislative determinations. (In reply to these questions, the Court declared without elaboration that "the required determinations fall within judicial competence.") At any rate, the justices could have reversed *Roe*'s moral conclusion about the relative value of these interests—or they could have decided that courts are not capable of making this kind of assessment—without reversing any legal principle. *Casey*, then, declined to overrule a legal principle established in the most criticized decision of our time only if the meaning of the term "legal principle" is stretched so far as to include moral conclusions about fiercely debated personal, political, medical, and spiritual questions.

Moreover, while the scope of the public's reliance on *Plessy* is clear and undeniable, the nature of the reliance interest in *Roe* is difficult to identify. The *Casey* Court actually toys with (but dismisses) the possibility that some women might engage in unprotected sexual activity based on the expectation that they could obtain an abortion if necessary. Reversing *Roe* would leave some of these women pregnant. But, again straying rather far from conventional legal issues, the Court goes on to note the improbability of people engaging in sexual behavior because of *Roe v. Wade* as well as the likelihood that "reproductive planning could take virtually immediate account of any sudden restoration of state authority to ban abortions."

The Court then considers the broader effect that the right to abortion has had on women's choices and understandings. The passage is worth examining:

> [F]or two decades of economic and social developments, people have organized intimate relationships and made choices that define their views of themselves and their places in society, in reliance on the availability of abortion.... The ability of women to participate equally in the economic and social life of the Nation has been facilitated by their ability to control their reproductive lives.

This rather self-congratulatory paragraph appears to be saying that the right to abortion furthered the emancipation of women by altering roles and values and, more concretely, by inducing women to enter into sexual relationships as well as into jobs. Of course, these changes were underway before *Roe* was decided in 1973 and were surely caused by many other factors besides the Court's decision. But even assuming *Roe* had a major part to play, how exactly would reversing *Roe* undermine any of this? Is the idea that women in the workforce would suddenly feel out of place because abortion was no longer available and that they would flee back to domesticity? Or that women who had entered into marriage or affairs because of the availability of abortion would suddenly regret their relationships?

The fact of the matter is that reversing *Roe* would not necessarily even eliminate the availability of abortion, since different states would presumably come to different judgments about how that procedure should be regulated. Consequently, reversing *Roe* might have no effect, or only minor effects, on women's expectations or behavioral patterns. Even on the assumption that abortion would be widely outlawed, the main consequences for women would be prospective, changing some decisions and attitudes and imposing some burdens. But it is difficult to see how past decisions made in reliance on *Roe* would be affected. Certainly, allowing states to regulate abortion again would not directly dismantle a pervasive social system, as overruling the doctrine of separate but equal did.

Neither the need to honor announced principles nor to protect entrenched expectations provides an explanation for giving the abortion decisions the status of super-precedents; in fact, both of these considerations suggest that *Roe* should have less precedential force than did *Plessy v. Ferguson*, which (as I have said) the Court is justly celebrated for overturning. Fortunately, other sections of the *Casey* opinion point us toward a fuller, if dismaying, understanding of why some of the justices think that the constitutional right to abortion should be set in cement.

Much of that opinion is concerned, one could say transfixed, with the fact that over the years much "political fire" has been directed at *Roe*. States had passed many statutes intended to test and limit the original abortion decision, the Justice Department had several times called on the Court to reverse that decision, and many political demonstrations (as well as some violence) had been directed at both the right of abortion and the Court responsible for it. At one level, this is a very odd reason for sticking with a precedent. Political fire, after all, is an indication that a significant number of people disagree with the Court's position on abortion. To an innocent mind, the fact that many people fervently think you are wrong is one reason to suspect that perhaps you are wrong.

The Court sometimes sees this logic or, at least a happy corollary. That is, it is inclined to see agreement as one reason to think its decisions are right. Recently, for instance, the Court refused to allow Congress to make changes in the regime of police warnings required by the once heavily criticized *Miranda* decision. The police, you see, had eventually come to accept the required procedures, and, indeed, the warnings had become accepted as "a part of our national culture." So, again, the obvious thought would be that judicial decisions that do not generate this kind of acceptance ought to have less precedential value. But the justices in *Casey* are more sophisticated than this and give a portentous reason why the fact of strong disagreement with *Roe* is a reason to refuse to overrule it.

If *Roe* were overturned, the country would, said the Court, "pay a terrible price." Because *Roe* resolved an "intensely divisive controversy" and, indeed, called the opposing sides in this controversy to "to end their ... division," reversing *Roe* would be seen by the general public as a "surrender to political pressure." In particular, many citizens—who had supported the right to abortion out of respect for the Court's authority and despite intense criticism of *Roe*—would feel betrayed by a reversal and naturally believe that the Court had capitulated to political pressure. Perceived as a political institution, the Court would lose legitimacy.

More ominously yet, since the American people's capacity to see themselves as living under the rule of law is tied to "their understanding of the Court invested with the authority to … speak before all others for their constitutional ideals," undermining the Court's legitimacy would threaten American constitutionalism and, in the end, the "Nation's commitment to the rule of law." Thus intense opposition to the original abortion decision becomes a reason, not to doubt that decision, but to reaffirm it. Our very nationhood depends on it.

No wonder Senator Specter asked if *Roe* were not now super-precedent. When asked about the weighty considerations discussed in *Casey*, nominee Alito replied blandly, "I think that the Court … should be insulated from public opinion. [Courts] should do what the law requires in all instances." But that is not precisely the argument made in *Casey*. In fact, *Casey* comes close to insisting on the opposite: that the Court should stay with a decision *wrongly* interpreting the Constitution because a reversal of that wrong decision would meet with public criticism and disapproval. Insofar as *Casey* rests on the relationship between judicial legitimacy and *stare decisis*, the Court is arguing that public opinion—in the form of attitudes about the Court—should trump law.

Of course, the *Casey* Court does not say outright that *Roe* was bad law. One would hardly expect that. But the justices do acknowledge the possibility that *Roe* might have been in error and they do refer to "the reservations [some justices] may have in reaffirming the central holding of *Roe*." And they do say that these reservations are overcome only by a reexamination of the constitutional questions involved "*combined with the force of stare decisis* [emphasis added]."

More disturbingly, *Casey* does not exactly say that following the precedent set by *Roe* is important in order to convince the public that the Court is in fact abiding by legal principle. More precisely, it says that it is important that the Court *appear* to be abiding by legal principle. Indeed, for all its high-toned references to the rule of law, the opinion is suffused with an implicit cynicism about the relationship between law and politics. At one point, for instance, it asserts that, because the usual reasons for overruling precedent do not apply to the original abortion decision, "the Court could not pretend to be reexamining the prior law with any justification beyond present doctrinal disposition to come out differently from the Court of 1973." *Pretend?* And since when is a considered judgment that a constitutional ruling was profoundly wrong as a matter of law been referred to as "a present doctrinal disposition to come out differently"?

More generally, in its discussion of judicial legitimacy, the Court refers to the perception of legality rather than the reality. For instance, it says, "There is a limit to the amount of error that can plausibly be imputed to prior Courts." Note: not the amount of error that might properly (as a matter of law) be imputed but the amount that might be made plausible to the public. *Casey* is concerned with the perception of legality more than the substance. Even as it declares that law must be separate from public opinion it elevates the public's opinion of the Court above law.

Casey's rather frantic concern for the Court's legitimacy is hard to explain. The justices had no evidence about the public's knowledge of the doctrine of precedent, no evidence that people think the Court seldom overrules prior decisions, and no evidence that the public loses respect for the Court when it does reverse a prior ruling. Moreover, it is not at all self-evident that the public thinks that constitutional decisions are immune from political considerations nor that this sort of realism would lead people to the conclusion that the Court is an illegitimate institution. It is quite possible, in fact, that among the general public the legitimacy of the Court is based partly on the belief that the judiciary does respond to politics and thus tends to produce results with which many people agree. It is certain that multitudes of lawyers, most law professors, and virtually all political scientists believe that the Court is influenced by political considerations. Few of these professionals, however, would describe it as illegitimate.

That *Casey's* fastidiousness about political influence on the Court should be invoked in a confirmation hearing is downright weird. Even as Senator Specter grilled Alito about the need to separate law and politics, he was engaged in a very public process whereby politicians, including Specter, were trying to affect the direction the Court would take. He was doing so at a time when the line between political considerations and legal considerations has largely vanished even in the way that the justices attempt to justify their judgments. And the doctrine that *Roe* is a super-precedent makes completely clear—as do scores of decisions that rest on precedent rather than on the Constitution itself—that the justices (and their defenders) now believe that the authority of the Court's decisions is more important than the authority of our fundamental law.

In short, the Court's position in *Casey* is that, while any source of authority in the legal mantra can normally be subordinated to any other, precedent prevails against all of them if the legitimacy of the Supreme Court is thought to be threatened. That is, despite the fact that the justices' personal beliefs can normally influence which source of legal authority should be dominant in a particular case, in a certain class of cases the justices' personal beliefs about the importance of their role require that the mantra be reduced to one word: precedent. Anyone still under "the lure of the next nominee" should consider how crucial to the American system lawyers believe the Supreme Court is and how unlikely it is that a Court populated by such lawyers will turn away from the deeply entrenched practice of pervasive intervention in the nation's affairs.

8

Political Judgments

When judges make the same kinds of judgments that legislators or executive branch officials do, the extralegal nature of the judgment is usually obscured by the formality and apparent precision of doctrinal language. In equal protection and due process cases, for example, the Court's terminology amounts to a ranking system. Some governmental purposes (say, in a case of racial discrimination) must be "compelling." Others (in a case of sex discrimination) need be only "important." (It was this difference that Senator Biden was referring to when he challenged Justice Rehnquist's criticism of those justices who wanted to establish the equivalent of an Equal Rights Amendment through interpretation.) Often all that must be demonstrated is "a legitimate interest." Below that level, some interests are categorized as "illegitimate" or even "invidious." Similarly, when the courts assess whether the government has chosen an appropriate method for achieving its goals, the linkage must sometimes be "necessary," sometimes "substantially related," and other times merely "reasonably related." Such terms take on the aura of legal categories even though they actually represent nothing different from ordinary moral or instrumental assessment.

Even when constitutional doctrines make no implicit claim for precision and accuracy, they are combined in such systematic ways that the impression created is juridical rather than political. Here, for example, is the "test" for deciding what process is constitutionally required before the government deprives a person of liberty or property:

> [O]ur prior decisions indicate that identification of the specific dictates of due process generally requires consideration of three distinct factors: First, the private interest that will be affected by the official action; second, the risk of an erroneous deprivation of such interest through the procedures used, and the probable value, if any, of additional or substitute procedural safeguards; and finally, the Government's interest, including the function involved and the fiscal and administrative burdens that the additional or substitute procedural requirement would entail.

The careful separation and delineation of all the factors to be taken into account lends an air of legalism, but the factors are exactly what any competent administrator or serious legislator would be considering when deciding what procedures to use in terminating welfare benefits or other government entitlements.

Lawyers are so accustomed to such doctrines that they seldom take note of the degree of overlap between legal judgment and executive or legislative judgment. The doctrines seem distinctively legal; in fact, operationally they constitute the constitutional "law" that law students learn and lawyers argue about. Aside from their familiarity and formality, there is another reason why judicial nominees and other sophisticated lawyers do not think that judges are invading the legislative or executive spheres when they utilize such doctrines. While executive branch officials and legislators sometimes do have reasons to justify the decisions they make, reason-giving is not the essence of their functions. As Bickel emphasized, political actors can usually act out of emotion or interest or guesswork. But it is thought to be the essence of judging that decisions are backed by reasons. Thus while the modern legal professional, when pressed, has to concede that in constitutional cases judges often do make the same kinds of judgments as those in the political branches, they think that judges make those judgments differently. All jurists, but especially the justices of the Supreme Court, must give reasons. So the essential difference between constitutional law and political judgment is thought to be that constitutional law represents reasoned judgment. Behind the judge's ruling is not just personal preference or experience—the self that virtually all judicial nominees agree cannot be left entirely behind when they ascend to the bench—but also (and mainly) something objective and reasoned.

The judicial ideal of reasoned judgment misapprehends how people, both politicians and judges, think about difficult public issues. The nature of this misapprehension can be seen in two major cases, both decided in 2003. One is *Grutter v. Bollinger* in which the Supreme Court found that diversity is a sufficiently compelling interest to justify the use of racial preferences in law school admissions. The other is *Lawrence v. Texas* in which the Court found that the moral disapproval of homosexual sodomy was not a sufficiently important interest to justify criminal prohibitions against such conduct.

Diversity as a Public Value

Let us begin with the affirmative action decision. Taken at face value, the *Grutter* Court's depiction of the values served by diversity in higher education is certainly attractive. Justice O'Connor begins by adverting to Justice Powell's idea that judicial respect for educational judgments about how best to achieve "a robust exchange of ideas" is grounded in notions of academic freedom and free speech.[1] She then expands on the range of educational advantages achieved through a racially diverse student body. Not only is classroom discussion "livelier, more spirited, and simply more enlightening," but also students learn about members of other races and, in the process, become skeptical of racial stereotypes. She says these are important educational benefits in their own right and also that they prepare students for later interactions in "an increasingly diverse workforce and society." In turn, the ability to operate in an interracial society is important to the functioning of major organizations, including businesses and the military. Indeed, participation by diverse groups in such organizations and in "civic life" more generally "is essential if the dream of one Nation, indivisible, is to be realized." The dream "of one Nation" is no idle abstraction either, for the opinion goes on to claim that the "legitimacy" of our social and governmental leadership requires that members of every race be represented in elite positions.

Diversity in higher education, then, serves not only specific educational purposes but also some of the same political purposes that the Supreme Court has on occasion claimed for its own work. Diversity, like certain constitutional decisions of the Court, is thought to stand as a bulwark against illegitimacy and fragmentation, or, put more affirmatively, as an embodiment of our aspirations for a just society. While the O'Connor opinion clings to Justice Powell's earlier rejection of the claim that making up for a diffuse history of racial discrimination is inadequate to justify racial preferences in higher education, it ends up embracing the more affirmative version of that goal. We may not look back to correct a history of hatred and inequality, but we may look forward to the achievement of harmony, cohesion, and evident fairness. How, you might well ask, could anyone doubt that all this represents a compelling public purpose?

The answer, of course, is that critics do not take these purposes at face value. They begin by denying that these are the actual purposes of the affirmative action program at the Michigan Law School. As the dissenters point out, racial preferences there seem to have counted just about enough to generate admission rates equivalent to the percentages in the applicant pool and, therefore, to attendance rates close to the same pro-

---

1.   Quoting *Regents of the Univ. of Cal. v. Bakke*, 438 U.S. 265, 312 (1978) (plurality opinion).

portion. This proportion, it is charged, bears no relationship to the laudable objectives asserted by the University. And it certainly would seem odd to believe that a critical mass of, say, 1 percent Native Americans in a class reflects the number necessary to vitalize class discussions and break down discredited stereotypes while a critical mass of 9 percent of African Americans is necessary to achieve the same result. Similarly, the necessity for lessons about how to interact with a particular race would seem to depend on the relative isolation of that race in society or the degree of prejudice held against it, not its proportion in the applicant pool. And the goal of political legitimacy might be achieved by (among other things) effective representation of the various races in leadership positions, but effectiveness is not guaranteed or even necessarily related to proportionality. More subtle preconditions for legitimacy—for example, Robert Post's suggestion that a democratic culture requires leaders who can both represent and transcend racial groups—have to do with attitudes and predispositions that, even if passed on in some subtle way through preferential admissions practices, are surely not related to proportionality. In short, the criticism is that the racial proportionality of programs like the one at the Michigan Law School reveals that they cannot, in fact, be aimed at their announced purposes.

Different critics see different purposes behind the design of affirmative action programs like Michigan's. One obvious possibility is that racial proportionality is a rough measure of what is necessary to redress a history of racial discrimination. And, indeed, the objective of correcting prior injustices makes some sense of the goal of racial proportionality. At least, at one time it was forthrightly argued that members of disadvantaged races should be represented in the classroom and in social intercourse and in leadership positions in roughly the same ratio as their percentage in the whole population because that is an approximation of the likely distribution that would have existed in the absence of a history of racial prejudice and discrimination.[2] The percentage of each race in the applicant pool may be the closest practical approximation of the percentage in the whole population. However, because the purpose of correcting historical inequities has been legally insufficient to justify racial preferences since

---

2.   Justice Brennan went so far as to argue that it was reasonable to conclude that but for pervasive racial discrimination, Bakke himself would not have qualified for admission to the Davis Medical School even in the absence of that school's special admission program. *Regents of the Univ. of Cal. v. Bakke*, 438 U.S. 265, 365-66 ((1978) (Brennan, J., concurring).

1977 when *Bakke* was decided, so goes the argument, schools have had to conceal their true objectives.

This criticism has considerable power. There can be no doubt that many affirmative action programs were originally undertaken to compensate for past discrimination; indeed, there are still voices in the academy insisting that this is their proper purpose. That purpose would also explain why diversity proponents are intensely worried about racial imbalances but often seem unconcerned about the absence from the classroom of other kinds of groups. (If advocates of racial diversity have ever pushed for admission of a critical mass of pro-life students or of religious fundamentalists or, for that matter, of anarchists, I, like many other observers, must have been absent that day.) For the same reasons, the objective of making up for past discrimination would explain why faculties devote so little time and attention to discussing or studying the actual effects of racial diversity on classroom discussion. And it also could help explain the anomaly that the diversity movement, along with its ideal of robust interchange, should have come into full flower during approximately the same period when many universities have undertaken strenuous efforts to sanitize discourse.

Still, even on the assumption that one main objective of most affirmative action admissions programs is the unspoken one of compensating for historical injustices, it does not follow that the acknowledged objectives are less than compelling. If for some reason it is true that correcting a history of racial discrimination is not a "compelling" purpose, the objective is not for that reason illegitimate. Programs motivated by remedial aims can also serve the kinds of purposes Justice O'Connor's opinion endorses. In fact, while it makes for some awkwardness and complexity, a program designed to achieve both a "compelling" purpose (like educational vigor) and a merely desirable purpose (like overcoming historical inequities) would seem, all other things being equal, more rather than less justified than one unequivocally aimed only at a single objective, even if that objective is thought to be compelling. If a governmental interest is in fact morally or politically important, I cannot see why it should become less so because it was not the proponents' original purpose or is not now their only purpose. Nor should it matter that it is not their primary purpose or even their real purpose. In such circumstances, the proponents might (to their critics) seem annoyingly opportunistic, perhaps even devious or hypocritical, but the moral worth of the government's interest is independent of the tactics or character of those who favor the interest.

This rather abstract response, of course, is persuasive only if the educational benefits of racial diversity are real and substantial. This the critics deny. And it must be acknowledged that the nature and extent of these benefits are highly questionable. The problem is not merely that empirical studies are provisional and, in any event, less than clear-cut. The problem is, as Peter Schuck and Peter Wood (among others) have argued, government programs aimed at generating diversity may undermine real diversity by making differences seem inauthentic and denatured. The problem goes further yet, for, as the *Grutter* opinion demonstrates, the idealistic purposes thought to justify racial preferences seem wholly independent of measurable outcomes. To begin with, consider the immediate educational benefits. Justice O'Connor's opinion contends that these include a robust exchange of ideas, but the opinion also insists that a robust exchange of ideas does not entail any assumption that minority students "always (or even consistently) express some characteristic minority viewpoint...." In fact, another educational benefit is that students discover that "such stereotypes" are untrue or at least that they have "diminish[ed] force." In a few highly nuanced sentences, then, the Court veers cheerfully from one possibility to another—(1) that minority group members have different enough experiences that they are more likely than others to provide certain ideas or perspectives that will be useful to classroom discussion, (2) that minority group members do not have identifiable viewpoints and that the elimination of such stereotypes is what makes their participation in classroom discussion so useful, and (3) that minority group members do have distinctive viewpoints—but only some of the time—and that the discovery that this is true is valuable because it reduces (or, one assumes, fine-tunes) racial stereotypes. In short, no matter what students learn from a racially diverse class, it is valuable.

This rather flexible line of thought, of course, could be extended. The Court, for example, suggests that racial diversity is educationally beneficial because it elicits strong exchanges of views, that is, that it increases the energy level of the discussion. But, if studies were to conclude that racial diversity in the classroom actually inhibits discussion (on, perhaps, at least some sensitive issues), then, of course, the very sense of inhibition could be said to be a valuable indicator of deep feelings and racial insecurities. Similarly, the Court alludes to the improved relationships among students of different races. But, if studies were to show that relationships (presumably, under some conditions) are made more competitive and hostile, then that very hostility might be said to be an important cautionary lesson.

Much the same is true of the more remote objectives approved by the Court. Students, it is claimed, must be prepared for interacting in a multiracial society. This preparation would be necessary if our institutions and organizations in fact turn out to be populated by many races and if the members of those races interact a great deal rather than self-segregate. In this instance, the benefit would arise because interracial understanding would allow participants to adjust to the happy circumstance of racial intermingling. But the preparation would also be necessary if some races were not proportionately represented in institutions and organizations or if the members tended towards non-cooperation and self-segregation. The benefit in this circumstance, of course, would arise because inter-racial understanding would allow participants to ameliorate or even overcome the unfortunate circumstance of racial isolation. Finally, it might be true that racial proportionality will increase the legitimacy of society's leadership because it might be true that people will see this pattern of representation as fair and effective. But if people do not see the pattern as fair and effective—if some see it as a spoils systems and others as a sign of the impossibility of achieving true political responsiveness in our system—then the resulting dissatisfaction still might be thought to be a pressing reason for diversity programs. After all, if legitimacy is in doubt under patterns of racially proportionate leadership, how much worse might the situation become under racially disproportionate patterns? The reality of racial participation at least holds the potential over time of convincing people that the system is, or is becoming, legitimate.

At first glance, this imperviousness to falsification would seem to be a crushing problem. It suggests that proponents want affirmative action programs whether or not the programs produce real diversity, indeed, no matter what their consequences. But wait. It is not so strange as it first sounds to say that a program that is good no matter what happens must be a very good program indeed. Consider a famous and influential example: John Stuart Mill, you may recall, argued that unwelcome opinions should not be silenced whether those opinions are wholly true, partly true, or entirely false. He argued that if wholly true, the expression of unwelcome opinions might help truth to emerge; if partly true, they can refine our understanding of what is true; and if false, they help prevent truth from becoming a dead dogma. Notice that Mill's argument still has force even if a true opinion is never accepted because his argument is only that tolerance makes the emergence of truth or partial truth *possible*.[3] Something similar can be said of the claim that without exposure to dissent, truth will become a dead dogma. This position does not require that every unwelcome opinion have the effect of making truth more vivid; it only requires that without continuing examination, truth will eventually become stale. Thus, Mill's argument holds not only without regard to how true the unwelcome opinion is, but also without regard to the actual outcome of debate. And the general conviction that untrammeled debate is good, no matter what its immediate consequences, is carried forward to the present day in highly respected and influential arguments for the open marketplace of ideas.

Mill's argument for tolerance is independent of immediate consequences because, ultimately, it presents an aspiration more than a prediction. The human capacity to reason about truth is mysterious; in some individuals and in some circumstances it is weak or nonexistent, while in others it is astonishingly potent. Mill's argument rests on the conjecture or the hope that the capacity for truth is sufficiently available that it is worth preserving the necessary preconditions for its attainment. Even if conditions were such that no human were rational enough either to communicate or appreciate truth, a follower of Mill might entertain the hope that conditions might change, or even that treating people as rational agents might help transform them into rational agents. And if met by the radical claim that no human in any circumstance can appreciate truth, a determined person might reply that this radical claim itself might eventually turn out to be false and it is on this hope that dissenting opinions should be tolerated. The conjectural, aspirational character of Mill's argument is a reflection of its scale and profundity, not a sign that its objective is unimportant.

Something similar, I think, can be said of the goals of racial diversity programs. It does not matter what specific lessons are learned from members of other races or—in particular circumstances—whether any lessons are learned at all, because without diversity there is less chance of learning anything from members of other races. It is not dispositive that we cannot be certain what the patterns of interaction will be in society at large because it is at least possible that these patterns, whether benign or hostile, will be improved by inter-racial experience at the university

---

3.   Mill wrote, "[W]e may hope that if there be a better truth, it will be found when the human mind is capable of receiving it." John Stuart Mill, *On Liberty*, 23 (quoted from the Haldeman-Julius edition, 1925.)

level. And, yes, the sources of political legitimacy are psychological and highly conjectural, but legitimacy is not for that reason less than crucial. In the end diversity is a compelling interest because of the ideals and hopes that it represents. Independent of its immediate consequences, racial proportionality is a tangible sign of inclusion, an expression of good faith, an embodiment of the desire for racial understanding and harmony. Diversity, then, is compelling to the extent that it expresses shared moral norms thought to be essential to a decent society.

Some of the most potent criticisms of affirmative action in university admissions concede—even celebrate—the attractiveness of diversity as a societal aspiration. Peter Schuck, for example, perceptively describes how cultural and attitudinal variety can make individual choices richer and social decisions more adaptive. Similarly, Peter Wood's colorful diatribe concedes (indeed, revels in) the excitement and usefulness of real diversity. "I don't know of anyone [says Wood] who argues that social 'uniformity' or ethnic 'homogeneity' make for better education or a more just society."

Schuck and Wood are nevertheless critics of government imposed racial diversity because they argue that it has significant costs, such as degraded discourse and individual unfairness, and that it actually undermines the attractive values of real (non-engineered) diversity. Now, it might be tempting to jump from the claim that a government program entails great cost and risk to the conclusion that its purpose cannot be "compelling" in the doctrinal sense. However, efforts to implement truly great public purposes will often be characterized by both high cost and risk because it is precisely the great governmental objectives that are thought to be important enough to justify large burdens and uncertainties. History, needless to say, is replete with various kinds of profoundly significant governmental initiatives—for example, strategies of military deterrence, educational reform measures, or the Supreme Court's edifice of free-speech protections for defamatory speech—that have been both burdensome and uncertain. Those who oppose racial preference programs on instrumental grounds may well be right in their bleak observations and dire predictions; they may be wiser or more prudent (at least in the short run) than those who support such programs. But even valid instrumental objections go to the best method for achieving a set of goals. They do not establish that the goals are politically unimportant or morally weak.

Nevertheless, it might be thought that engineered diversity cannot be a compelling purpose (in the doctrinal sense) if there is a less risky, less costly way to achieve the desired objectives.[4] In effect, the Court adopts this view when it asks whether racial diversity can be achieved without specific forms or degrees of racial preference. Surely, it might be thought, a program cannot have a compelling justification if its goals could be achieved in a different, less troublesome way. But, again, this argument has force only if the goals of diversity are understood as narrowly instrumental. It is, of course, true that some amount of racial diversity would exist in higher education without any racial preferences in admissions. It is also true, as the *Grutter* dissenters charge, that students can and do learn about attitudes associated with minority experiences long before they come to law school. And even in law school, students can be assigned books about the minority experience and, indeed, whole courses can be designed to meet this need. Students can visit or work in minority neighborhoods. Later, racial harmony in the workplace can be achieved the same way most work-related skills are achieved—through on-the-job training and, assuming that racial animosities are costly and unpleasant, through the operation of ordinary incentives and experiences. The moral and political legitimacy of society's leadership can be established in part through visibly fair competition and through responsive, transparent institutions. These suggestions for alternatives to racial proportionality are not trivial or artificial. In fact, against the great tides of practical experience, economic reality, and political life that move outside the law school classroom, racial diversity in university classrooms might well be only a small eddy.

But none of the alternative methods for achieving racial understanding and harmony achieves the expressive purposes inherent in diversity programs based on racial preferences. For one thing, most of the alternative methods, even if effective in some ways, are not purposeful collective actions and therefore cannot embody shared moral commitments. Even those alternatives, like courses designed to educate on racial history and experience, that are purposeful do not involve the same sacrifices as do diversity programs and therefore do not express the same level of moral conviction and determination.

To summarize, then, the criticisms leveled at diversity do establish, I think, that it is not a compelling public objective in any immediate, instrumental sense. But the importance and power of diversity do not

---

4.   I recognize, of course, the Court's formulations separate under different "prongs" the issue of the importance of the purpose and the issue of "less drastic means," as if they were unrelated to one another.

depend on achieving specific, measurable consequences. Diversity is compelling because it represents and expresses a defining aspiration. It is defining in the sense that its pursuit is pivotal to a vast array of public choices and, ultimately, to society's fundamental conception of its own morality.

To acknowledge that diversity is a compelling purpose in this sense does not at all imply that it is beyond doubt even as an aspiration. Not only are some of its immediate effects objectionable and its long-run consequences speculative, more fundamentally the underlying moral vision is itself controversial if only because it is premised on race-consciousness. The dream of a color-blind society, where every individual's value is independent of race, is (needless to say) also profoundly compelling. That is why the Court, even as it upheld Michigan's affirmative action program, indicated that such programs should end in twenty-five years. The very ambivalence in the Court's diversity opinions represents a recognition that on the great questions of social and political direction, various goals, even opposite ones, can represent powerful moral commitments and that the public is entitled to choose.

Sexual Morality as a Public Value

I suspect that some who strongly approve of the Court's decision in *Grutter* will nevertheless be uneasy with my account of why diversity is a compelling public interest. The reason for this unease is not hard to identify. If an interest as diffuse, costly, uncertain, and controversial as diversity is important enough to permit government to override an individual's liberty interest, there may be a very broad range of objectives that justifies restrictions on liberty. This possibility, it seems to me, is not a reason to simplify or distort our understanding of why diversity is a compelling interest. Rather, it is a reason to think further about what it means to judge the importance of a public purpose.

Consider the nature of the states' interest in regulating private sexual conduct, an issue that the Supreme Court happens to have taken up at almost the same time that it was assessing the importance of racial diversity at the University of Michigan Law School. In *Lawrence v. Texas*, the Court concluded that a criminal prohibition against private homosexual conduct "furthers no legitimate interest which can justify … intrusion into the personal and private life of the individual." A cursory reading of this sentence might leave the impression that the justices are asserting that the state has no legitimate interest in regulating private sexual conduct. But the phrasing actually suggests that Texas does have such an interest and that the problem is that its interest, legitimate as it may be, is not strong enough to justify a particular degree of intrusion into the right to privacy. Elsewhere the opinion acknowledges the nature of the state's legitimate interest:

> [F]or centuries there have been powerful voices to condemn homosexual conduct as immoral. The condemnation has been shaped by religious beliefs, conceptions of right and acceptable behavior, and respect for the traditional family. For many persons these are not trivial concerns but profound and deep convictions accepted as ethical and moral principles to which they aspire and which thus determine the course of their lives.

The Court goes quickly on to say that "[t]hese considerations do not answer the question before us" because the issue is whether this moral position may be enforced "on the whole society through operation of the criminal law."

And it is true that the legitimacy of the state's moral position is not, given the Court's balancing paradigm, wholly determinative of the constitutional issue, since any balance would also have to take into account the degree of deprivation of the right to privacy. But it is equally true that the importance of that moral interest is not wholly irrelevant either since (as we certainly know from *Grutter*) even core constitutional interests of an individual can be sacrificed for a sufficiently important governmental purpose. So, the question cannot be avoided: If we grant that diversity in higher education is a compelling governmental interest, is there any basis for denying that status to the moral objectives that animate prohibitions against homosexual conduct?

The *Lawrence* majority suggests one answer even as it describes Texas' moral position respectfully. Listen again to its words: "For many persons," [the state's moral position reflects] profound and deep convictions accepted as ethical and moral principles to which they aspire and which thus determine the course of their lives." This phrasing suggests that the moral principles animating the Texas prohibition are entitled to respect because their proponents use them in shaping their own hopes and choices. They are, the phrasing implies, important expressions of morality for the private domain but not for the public arena. Thus, if the Court had felt called upon to reconcile its assessment of the moral interest in suppressing homosexual behavior with its assessment of the government's interest in racial diversity, it could have noted that those who support diversity in higher education are pursuing a moral vision of public life—a vision of how law school classes should function, of how the races should interact in businesses and other organizations, and of how society's leadership can earn legitimacy.

The decisive answer to this distinction between private and public spheres was provided long ago in Ronald Dworkin's "reconstruction" (as he called it) of Lord Devlin's argument in favor of moral regulation. Dworkin's reading of Devlin is worth hearing:

> If those who have homosexual desires freely indulged them, our social environment would change. What the changes would be cannot be calculated with any precision, but it is plausible to suppose ... that the position of the family, as the assumed and natural institution around which the education, economic and recreational arrangements of men center, would be undermined.... We are too sophisticated to suppose that the effects of an increase in homosexuality would be confined to those who participate in the practice ... , just as we are too sophisticated to suppose that prices and wages affect only those who negotiate them. The environment in which we and our children must live is determined ... by patterns and relationships formed privately by others than ourselves.

Notice that this version of Devlin's argument does not depend on any demonstration that homosexual conduct is in itself immoral. It could be, as the *Lawrence* Court repeatedly asserts, that judgments about private sexual morality must be made by individuals or even that homosexual conduct is at least sometimes a moral good; nevertheless Devlin would still be right that permitting this conduct could lead to public harms. The right to negotiate a twelve-hour workday (or, for that matter, to gain admission to the Michigan Law School on a race-neutral basis) is not in itself immoral, yet the exercise of these private rights can frustrate legitimate public purposes.

Dworkin's sympathetic account of Devlin's argument does not mean that he accepts Devlin's conclusions. Dworkin attempts to rebut Devlin's argument on its own terms.[5] He claims that Devlin recognizes that the

---

5. Dworkin's choice of counter-argument does not mean, of course, that there are no other possible critiques of Devlin's position. Dworkin mentions in passing several other possible lines of attack—that society is not entitled at all to protect itself from a change in social institutions, or (more modestly) that the threatened change must be imminent, or that the immorality of an act ought not to count "in determining whether to make it criminal," or that legislators must make the moral judgment for themselves and "not refer such issues to the community at large." 75 *Yale L. J.* at 993-94. Given Dworkin's later writings, it is also worthwhile to mention the argument that moral condemnation cannot be based on religious conviction. See, e.g., *Life's Dominion* (1993). Only the first two of these claims could be dispositive of Devlin's argument (as Dworkin's describes that argument), since moral condemnation is only necessary as a justification when the value of the social institutions at risk is not clear. It is hard to imagine the basis for an

legislator's decision to protect social institutions from private conduct is a difficult one, since the legislator must decide "whether the institutions which seem threatened are sufficiently valuable to protect at the cost of human freedom." The legislator, however, can proceed with some confidence when the private behavior is immoral because in that case there is less need for a strong public justification. Dworkin, with characteristic self-assurance, proceeds to argue that the moral position condemning private homosexuality does not meet minimal social standards regarding moral reasoning.

Dworkin's criticism, even if convincing as far at goes, is plainly an incomplete reply to Devlin's argument as Dworkin himself describes that argument. Unaccountably, Dworkin loses sight of his own recognition that Devlin's position does not require that private conduct always be immoral in order to justify public regulation.[6] It follows from Dworkin's account of Devlin that it is possible for a legislator to be confident that threatened social institutions are highly valuable and that in such circumstances the cost in human freedom might be worthwhile whether or not the regulated behavior is immoral. Dworkin simply assumes that the institutions threatened by repealing anti-sodomy laws are not so clearly valuable as to make judgments about the morality of homosexuality unnecessary.

To summarize, Dworkin's discussion shows that the question whether there is a compelling public purpose in prohibiting private homosexual conduct is not answered by distinguishing between the private and public spheres and is logically separate from the question whether the private conduct is moral or not. If the importance of the governmental interest is to be assessed, there is simply no escaping the need to identify and evaluate the social institutions that may be threatened by legalizing homosexual acts.

---

argument that society is never entitled to protect itself from a destructive change in social institutions. It is possible to imagine an argument for the proposition that the change must be imminent, but surely such arguments lose force to the extent that the value of the endangered social institutions is great. The Court in *Grutter* imposed no requirement that serious risks, such as the gradual loss of governmental legitimacy, be imminent. The family, too, one would think, is a sufficiently valuable institution to warrant protection from remote risks. *See p. 117, infra.*

6   Dworkin's words are: "We do not need so strong a justification, in terms of the social importance of the institutions being protected, if we are confident that no one has a moral right to do what we want to prohibit.... This does not claim that immorality is sufficient to make conduct criminal; it argues, rather, that *on occasion* it is necessary." *Id.* at 993 [emphasis added].

The *Lawrence* Court, to its credit, makes more of an effort at this essential inquiry than does Dworkin. It points to various pieces of evidence that suggest that there is not a strong social consensus in favor of outlawing private homosexual acts. This information is certainly relevant to an assessment of the importance of the state's interest because to the extent that a society does not aspire to the sorts of relationships, institutions, and ideals that would be undermined by legalized homosexuality, that society would not be threatened by such legalization. However, if we agree with the Court that racial diversity in higher education is a compelling governmental interest, it is obvious that significant social dissensus cannot in itself be sufficient to discredit a public purpose. After all, the value of diversity programs is hotly contested in the political arena, and, indeed, those programs are arguably incompatible with a powerful, authoritatively expressed political consensus in favor of non-discrimination. *Grutter* is, I think, commonsensical on this point. Whatever the ultimate boundaries of Devlin's argument for the right of societal self-definition, it cannot be that a state's purposes are compelling only when they are non-controversial. The great issues of politics and morality are always controversial.

Fortunately, for present purposes it is not important to identify the degree of consensus that Devlin's argument might require before the state undertakes moral regulation on profound and controversial issues. Whatever the abstract answer to that question, in *Lawrence* the justices effectively concede that there is sufficient social consensus about the importance of at least one of the institutions thought to be threatened by legalized homosexuality. Both the majority opinion and Justice O'Connor's concurring opinion sharply distinguish criminal prohibitions against homosexuality from the validity of existing laws regulating marriage. And well they might, for marriage is the primary institution that has been used all over the world to tame the turbulent power of human sexuality, to raise psychologically healthy children, to instill moral values, and to provide for some degree of mutual protection and support. Whatever its variations and shortcomings, if there is not sufficient social consensus regarding the importance of the institution of heterosexual marriage, it is hard to imagine any social arrangement the protection of which could amount to a compelling interest. This is true notwithstanding the existence of alternative models to traditional marriage that are morally attractive and compatible with homosexuality. A public purpose does not cease to be compelling merely because deeply attractive alternatives exist, as

Grutter's acknowledgement of the dream of a colorblind society as an alternative to engineered diversity reminds us.

Lawrence might be thought to rest on the belief that the state's interest in protecting the institution of marriage, while morally compelling, is only tenuously connected to the prohibited conduct. Many have argued (and the Court seems to have been sure) that legalizing homosexual sodomy will not lead to any destructive consequences for family life. Indeed, arguments are available for the proposition that even extending the right to marry to homosexuals (let alone decriminalizing homosexual conduct) would be compatible with wholesome family life. Once again, however, this explanation for *Lawrence* is undermined by the Court's determination in *Grutter* that racial diversity in higher education is a compelling public purpose. You might recall that every aspect of that purpose—the invigoration of classroom discussion, the improvement of racial attitudes, the achievement of harmony in the workplace, the legitimation of the leadership class—is highly conjectural and, indeed, that diversity can be and is viewed as a compelling interest no matter what the immediate consequences. The *Grutter* opinion rests on the proposition that great dreams, like the aspiration for racial harmony and fairness, are sufficiently crucial to a society's self-definition that they can be worth expressing and pursuing despite the uncertainties that attend social causation in a complex and subtle world.

Even if legalized homosexuality might have some effect on social climate that could indirectly undermine marriage, it is, obviously, possible to protect marriage by more direct means than though the regulation of homosexual behavior. *Grutter*, however, also reminds us that the fact that certain tangible objectives might be achieved by more direct or limited means does not make the expressive functions of public laws any the less crucial to a society that ultimately reflects the character and attitudes of those who comprise it.

The Court's determination that racial diversity in higher education is a compelling interest is, I have tried to demonstrate, persuasive, but it is persuasive only on terms that confirm what should have been obvious from the beginning. What should have been obvious is that the nature of great social purposes is such that they cannot be authoritatively ranked by judges or, for that matter, by anyone else. They are the appropriate subject matter of continuing disagreement. Controversy, uncertainty, speculation, sacrifice—these do not make purposes unimportant. They identify ideals, they characterize dreams.

Much more is at stake in recognizing this than the decisions on racial diversity and private homosexual conduct. We Americans have become inured to a practice that is, I think, beyond justification. That practice is the supposedly reasoned ranking by the courts of the importance of public purposes. The practice reaches very far—it constrains our efforts to establish decent public dialogue, to maintain confidence in the electoral system, to redress a history of racial discrimination, and to foster a minimal sense of respect for our country. The practice is unjustified because the kinds of reasons that animate controversial public objectives are not objective. They are inseparable from individual identity, from experience and expression and hope. Judges, when making these judgments as a matter of constitutional law, have no other reasons to give than are available to everyone else.

9

Training, Experience, and Instinct

Until now I have been discussing how modern lawyers think about constitutional law. My chief claim has been that these intellectual patterns and resources provide no brakes on the judiciary's excessive use of its power and, indeed, that they are a cause of that excess. To put it another way, I have been saying that the way lawyers think about constitutional law makes it virtually impossible to turn the Court from its interventionist course. My examination of the dominant understanding of constitutional law and judicial role has included a number of observations about the interplay between modern interpretive norms and judicial temperament, but it is time to broaden the focus beyond legal philosophy to consider the effects on character and instinct of the experience of being part of the legal profession.

It is important to acknowledge that, of course, lawyers come in all types. Some, no doubt, are mild, retiring, and kindly. But, as the stereotype holds, many are self-confident, aggressive, and dominating. Moreover, there are some commonalities to the educational and professional experiences of the successful lawyers who become judges, especially federal judges and most especially justices of the Supreme Court. These commonalities, I will be suggesting, tend to create certain inclinations no matter what the underlying personality type might be. To hope that lawyers who have been highly successful in their legal education and practice will restrain themselves in the use of power is, well, whistling in a gale.

Intellect in Legal Training and Practice

At its best and highest levels, both legal education and the practice of law involve the imposition of order on complex factual disputes and the marshalling of rational arguments. It is a profession that honors detachment, discipline, intellect, and, above all, words. As valuable as these aspirations and tools can be, those who strive for them in their daily work can easily become distrustful or even disdainful of the political process because that process involves unruly conflict, raw power, and emotionality. In politics the strongest arguments do not always prevail, and words are sometimes less important than experience; failure, disorder, and even disaster are always possibilities. Consequently, judges, who occupy an even more controlled environment than do practicing lawyers, will often view the outcomes of the political process as irrational, unjustifiable, or excessively risky. This is another reason, then, that it was natural for the Court to intervene in the Florida election controversy of 2000 or to see political resistance to *Roe v. Wade* as profoundly illegitimate. It is also a reason that the justices tend to rely on elite opinion as expressed in the official positions of professional associations and university leaders, or to credit social science research and international treaties. When such materials conflict with the less exalted opinions that can influence political decision making, the Court's constitutional rulings will tend to dismiss those political decisions.

The idea that judicial decisions constitute a superior domain of rational thought is inherent in the methods of legal education. Every day in law school classrooms across the country thousands of students are asked to evaluate the decisions of appellate courts by articulating—and then either attacking or defending—the various legal positions taken in those cases. In theory the point of this exercise is for subsequent questioning to reveal to students potential weaknesses in their thinking and to initiate students into the sometimes subtle parameters of lawyerly argumentation.

This so-called Socratic method, however, inevitably teaches a number of different lessons as well. Because so much depends on the evaluation of judges' work, the esoteric language of the law takes on almost magical qualities even in this age of realism. It is, after all, the mastery of this language that determines not only justice in the particular case but often (as we saw in the last chapter) the proper direction of social policy or the correct outcome of moral debate. The power of lawyers' words is even more magical because the cases themselves necessarily simplify highly complex factual circumstances and, indeed, the students' evaluation of the cases (truth be told) is frequently not based on extensive thought or reading. Indeed, the judicial doctrines and the lawyerly arguments are largely barren of any sophistication in empirical research or policy analysis or historical study or moral discourse. So it seems to the student that this art of argumentation, at least when combined with quick intelligence (and perhaps a patina of familiarity with the social sciences), can—must!—make up for profound deficiencies in knowledge and effort.

The intense concentration on the language of appellate cases helps to make this extraordinary potential seem plausible to the student, especially since judicial language (as we also saw in the last chapter) typically employs a kind of all-purpose instrumentalism that is reassuringly modern and superficially enlightened. But some anxiety necessarily underlies the students' growing excitement about the power of the lawyers' craft. For one thing, since every argument is met with another argument and since convincing majority opinions are met with an equally convincing dissent, "the law" seems disquietingly plastic and possibly even arbitrary. The law student can take away from this both high aspiration (since the future is there to be shaped by argument) and insecurity (since adversarial methods open endless vistas of argumentation). In this combination, often, are planted the seeds of boundless ambition and dogged, sometimes closed-minded, devotion to legal methodologies and judicial authority.

The argumentative discussion of appellate decisions that lies at the heart of legal education teaches another, perhaps even more basic, lesson. As students watch each other struggle to avoid intellectual embarrassment or defeat, they learn to admire the capacity to argue for its own sake. In recent years this implicit lesson has become more powerful because standards of political correctness and the right of students to evaluate their teachers make it difficult for professors to ask the kinds of follow-up questions that might lead to real insight and growth. As a result, the tendency to invest argumentation with moral status increasingly lacks humility or self-doubt.

As admirable as it is in some ways, then, legal education breeds and dignifies some dangerous inclinations. It encourages people to favor constructed, simplified, or imagined idealizations over real life. It encourages excessive pride in skill at manipulating a professionalized vocabulary, a vocabulary from which the general public is by definition disqualified. And it confuses the skills of argumentation with morality itself.

All of these tendencies can be seen in the debilitating after-effects of the 2000 Florida election decision. After *Bush v. Gore,* it has become an article of faith, especially among Democratic Party lawyers—and, through them, among party activists—that President Bush's election was illegitimate. For years now this belief and rhetoric has helped to poison politics. And it has led to the regular deployment of armies of lawyers, prepared to litigate any closely contested election—a habit that could eventually undermine orderly transitions of presidential authority.

What makes this highly risky and destructive behavior truly puzzling is that widely reported, independent reviews of the Florida ballots indicate that Bush would have won if the general recount ordered by the Florida Supreme Court had been allowed to go forward and even if the highly selective recount requested by Gore had been carried out. Given this evidence and given what is at stake for our constitutional system, why do so many Democratic lawyers (not to mention law school professors) cling to their conviction that the Florida election was stolen?

The answer to this question, I think, goes back to legal education and practice. Consider one aspect of the Florida election myth that has some basis in reality. It may well be that more people in Florida intended to vote for Gore than for Bush and that Bush's victory was based on mistakes in marking ballots. To the extent that this is the basis for charges of illegitimacy, the facts do not matter because the outrage is not based on how the marked ballots were counted, but on the failure of the marked ballots to reflect true intentions. But to what kind of mind is it a profound injustice that some voters either did not have the intention that is now somehow attributed to them or, if they did, failed to implement that intention? It is an injustice to an idealist for whom abstractions matter more than actual behavior. Legal advocates construct an imagined ideal voter and rage against the reality of the actual counted votes.

Now consider another fact-based foundation for the Florida myth. The Electoral College votes from Florida were credited to Bush after the United States Supreme Court rejected the arguments of Gore's lawyers. Those arguments were forcefully made and, as many law professors have since written, the Court may have been wrong in rejecting them. But all controversial cases involve the rejection of strong arguments. In any event, it now appears that Gore would have lost the Florida vote even if his arguments had been accepted. To what kind of mind is it a severe injustice that an argument is rejected even if that argument could not have changed anything? It matters to the kind of mind for which the making of an argument in itself has urgent moral force.

Once again, Ronald Dworkin's writings illustrate—at a suitably high level of intellectualization—lawyers' instincts, in this case a reckless unconcern for reality. Remember, to begin with, his odd insistence that, as a matter of interpretation, the Bork confirmation hearings represented the nation's rejection of Bork's emphasis on original intent and its acceptance of Dworkin's own jurisprudence of principle—despite his acknowledgment that the hearings did not measure the actual beliefs of a majority of Americans. More broadly, a basic part of Dworkin's legal philosophy is his insistence that constitutional rights should be defined in large measure according to abstract philosophical inquiry, quite independently of the actual impact that the exercise of those rights will have on society.

Judging without Facts

Judges are not free to be as outspoken as philosophers are, and so they do not openly embrace the bottom line of Dworkin's theorizing. In fact, precise and systematic attention to facts is a point of pride to jurists, as it is to high quality attorneys. Nevertheless in Supreme Court opinions there is often a garish dissonance between the justices's lofty concerns about justice and the miserable reality that actually gave rise to the case. Think, for instance, of *Roper v. Simmons* (2005), in which the Court struck down laws in twenty states that had permitted the death penalty for murderers who committed their crime while 17 years of age. This decision was greeted with the usual stirrings of admiration and excitement on National Public Radio and in other organs of respectable commentary.

The case, however, involved a young man named Christopher Simmons, whose crime was the occasion for Justice Kennedy's musings about "the dignity of all persons" and "the evolving standards of decency." Simmons had told people he wanted to commit a murder and enticed two friends into his plan for murder in part by assuring them that as juveniles they would "get away with it." He then committed that murder by breaking into a home at 2:00 AM, binding a woman with duct tape and electrical wire, and throwing her from a railroad bridge into the river below. All this is calmly recounted by the justices before they proceed to ruminate—without irony—about the difficulties of deciding whether a juvenile offender is especially blameworthy. This construction of an edifice of enlightened theorizing over a base of sordid facts is nothing new. Blasé disregard for brutality is apparent, for example, in cases establishing a right to partial birth abortion and invalidating efforts to protect the privacy of rape victims.

Virtually every other aspect of the *Roper* decision is also now routine: the happy insistence that the meaning of the Constitution "evolves"; the confident assertion that the nature of this evolution is ultimately a matter for the Court's "own independent judgment"; the reliance on elite opinion as expressed in social science research or international law; the distrust of popular decision making institutions like juries; the opportunistic departure from prior rulings (in this case, a decision rendered only 15 years earlier); the blithe willingness to settle under the mantle of legal principle questions, like the age of maturity, that are inherently unprincipled matters of degree; the nationalization of issues once left to the states and the judicialization of policy decisions once thought to be legislative. All this is normal practice. The justices, caught up in abstractions about human dignity and elaborate arguments about the age of maturity, do not even seem to be aware of the extraordinary hubris exhibited in their decision. It is all in a day's work.

People who succeed in (and, later, preside over) the difficult task of adversarial argument are not inclined to self-doubt. They have learned from the first day of law school to be assertive and then to be self-confident. The notion that a high level lawyer or judge might not be more competent than others to decide matters of public policy is also undermined by the fact that lawyers and judges tend to be generalists. They have had the experience of conquering difficult material on anything from the economics involved in anti-trust cases to the medical details necessary to try a malpractice case. There is, of course, great potential value in the generalist's perspective, for an outsider can bring both skepticism and creativity to decision making that is normally the province of specialists. But it carries its own risks, as well. One of those risks is overconfidence and the resulting willingness to decide matters about which the generalist is actually ignorant.

A shocking illustration is the famous *Pentagon Papers* decision (1971). In this case, the justices were faced with executive branch claims that printing newspaper articles exposing an extensive and classified history of the Vietnam War would do great harm. These claims included the possible disclosure of military plans and the identity of spies, not to mention weakening the nation's alliances and prolonging the war. The Court declined to prevent publication largely on the ground that the government had not demonstrated sufficient danger. In itself, this result is not necessarily dismaying. But what is dismaying is the fact that the justices came to this conclusion without having studied—much less having had experts analyze—the forty-seven volumes at issue. Before oral argument was held, most of the justices had never even visited the room where the papers were being kept. Indeed, Erwin Griswold, representing the government at that argument, had not had time to read the documents. The case was effectively decided within a day or so after the argument, so there was no opportunity for any of the justices to study the massive report.

Whether the justices' guess about the risk of harm from disseminating the *Pentagon Papers* turned out to be right or wrong, the simple fact is that they were willing to decide matters of great complexity and urgency in a state of substantial ignorance. In such a state it was not difficult to dismiss, as several did, dangers that (while possibly extremely serious) might be somewhat remote or uncertain. If the majority had said that the right to freedom of speech requires that the public accept the risk of any and all harms resulting from the publication of classified information, its extreme haste would have been unwise but legally irrelevant. Instead, the justices convinced themselves that they were able to evaluate the danger to national security on the basis of, at best, superficial familiarity with the documents at issue.

Many legal analysts regard the justices' haste in the *Pentagon Papers* case as having limited significance because it was a consequence of the government's unusual effort to prevent publication (as opposed to punishing it afterwards). But the Court is often cavalier in its judgments about harm to the public. A much more ordinary case decided in 2001, illustrates the point. In *Bartnicki v. Vopper* the Court held that under certain conditions it violates freedom of speech to impose money damages on a person who broadcasts the contents of an illegally intercepted cellular telephone conversation. The Court had to acknowledge that, as Congress had found, publicizing such conversations would do serious harm to private relationships, including harm to the development of ideas that takes place in private discussions. Nevertheless, the Court declared that this privacy interest is less important than the public's need for information on a matter of public concern. The justices, however, had no way of knowing how much harm to private relationships would be done by disclosures of this sort and hardly pretended to know. Nor did the Court have any way of knowing how much important information would be unavailable for public debate if a remedy for disclosure were allowed. They were not in fact balancing anything. They were, once again, guessing about matters of high importance and, in the process, were willing to put aside the considered judgment of Congress.

Judges are under considerable pressure to believe that they are well informed and competent even when they are acting in ignorance. After all, their jobs require them to make difficult decisions across an impossibly wide range of issues. Put yourself in the judge's position. To indulge in self-doubt would be to entertain the possibility that you may have made serious blunders in case after case and, indeed, that no one is capable of doing the tasks that you have signed on to do. It is only natural to assume you are capable of doing what you believe you have to do. This assumption is fortified by the fact that each judge knows that around the country legions of other judges are confidently substituting their judgments for the judgments of public officials of all sorts.

The lawyers' culture of abstraction and adversarial argumentation is, then, reinforced by the tradition of lawyer-as-generalist. There are other professional and institutional reasons that increase the chances of heedless confidence. The first of these is that judges, especially Supreme Court justices, are responsible for carrying out highly important tasks and are keenly aware of this fact. Judges view themselves as being responsible for upholding the rule of law. The importance of this and other judicial tasks means that the imposition of costs and risks on others can sometimes be experienced as a virtue, as when a judge resolutely enforces the exclusionary rule by freeing a criminal. Similarly, the willingness to expose the nation to serious risk of harm in *Pentagon Papers* was a sign of the high importance of freedom of speech and of the Court's central role in protecting it.

A second reason for judicial self-confidence is that because they operate in an adversarial system judges are accustomed to a rather passive role. It is the responsibility of the lawyers in a case to bring forward the relevant evidence and to make the relevant arguments. Judges sit back and hear one argument or account of events set against another. Much of their work, that is, depends on evaluating what is presented to them. Therefore, it is natural for a judge to come to think that it is the responsibility of others to articulate and to persuade; if the argument is not made or the data is not produced, it does not go into the court's opinion. Adversarial instincts can thus lead judges to conflate the quality of an advocate's performance with truth. The government's chief lawyer in *Pentagon Papers* may not have been in a position to argue persuasively about the dangers represented by publication, but the Court was habituated to plunging ahead to decide on the basis of what was presented to it. The great welter of information out in the world that never makes it into the courtroom does not, in a sense, exist.

A third reason is that judges sit in constant review of claims that government has failed in some way. Official omissions and mistakes are the gist of innumerable lawsuits. This tends to induce in judges a bleak assessment of the performance and credibility of government officials, and the result is to increase the judge's distrust and even disdain for judgments made in the political branches.

Fourth, while the judicial role is highly significant, judges do not view themselves as having primary responsibility for setting or implementing public policy. To a degree, they think of themselves as bystanders or (in the phrasing John Roberts used in his confirmation hearing) referees and not players. This can lead to unrealistic expectations about those bold enough to be primary players. From the sidelines it is easy, not only to distrust the judgments of those who hold the central levers of power, but at the same time to think that these powerful people *should* be able to head off damage or minimize risk. And if, for instance, publication of the *Pentagon Papers* had led to prolongation of the Vietnam War, the finger of responsibility would have been pointed at those with primary responsibility for foreign affairs. The justices, who earlier had claimed for themselves the authority to assess danger to the nation, would by then have been again off center stage.

The Fetish of the Case

A final consideration is the lawyer's understandable fascination with cases. Make no mistake, although lawyers do many kinds of tasks, the case is the paradigmatic legal event. As I have said, despite some movement in law schools to break out of the confines of teaching from appellate opinions, most legal education still is centered on judges and how they resolve particular cases. Needless to say, the litigation of cases is one of the main components of the practice of law. And today, with so many distinctions between judicial and political functions broken down, there is a solid consensus among lawyers that the judicial function is different from the political in that judges only decide cases and, then, only the cases brought before them.

Perversely, the idea that judges can only decide cases as they arise has a liberating effect. One reason for this is that the judge can view the task at hand as having been imposed rather than sought. *I didn't ask to decide this issue—the case was thrust upon me!* At the level of the Supreme Court this self-image in almost entirely fictional, since for the most part the justices pick and choose which cases to hear. Nevertheless, it is a hallowed aspect of the common-law tradition that judges are obligated to decide the cases that are presented, and the psychological residue of this tradition still, I suspect, encourages the justices to view themselves as passive, even beleaguered, functionaries.

Moreover, the focus on the single case, especially when accompanied by the conservative instincts to resolve as little as necessary and to ground the decision in the specific facts of the case, can embolden a judge. *There is no reason to avoid this issue because, after all, I am not laying down any broad rule and even the holding in this case can be avoided in the future if new factual variations arise.* Thus a minimalist position can encourage intervention. Moreover, as Justice Scalia has pointed out, in some ways minimalism actually increases the discretion of the judge because so much depends, not on the application of a rule, but on the judge's assessment of circumstances. Finally, in deciding very little, a judge rules out very little. Hence, at the extreme every variation on governmental policy can be brought before the judicial forum; cumulatively the result is a kind of roving judicial supervision.

There is also a more subtle dynamic at play. Since a judge is restrained by the fact that the judicial role is limited to deciding particular cases and since there lingers in the air the old common-law tradition that a judge is obligated to decide cases presented, lawyers tend to slide to the conclusion that legal resources must authoritatively resolve all cases. In constitutional cases, this translates into an unspoken assumption that the Constitution must provide the answer to any societal dispute. After all, the dispute has been presented as a case and the case must be resolved; moreover, in resolving the case the judge is within the judicial function because only a case is being decided. In short, it is increasingly difficult for the modern legal mind to imagine any alternative to the pervasive and aggressive use of judicial power that we have become so accustomed to in the modern era.

This odd phenomenon is nicely illustrated by the argument, which has been advanced by some law professors, that there is no exit from judicial involvement in abortion policy. Even if the Court were to overrule *Roe v. Wade*, so goes the argument, it would have to resolve any number of abortion-related questions that would pop up after *Roe* was overturned. It is also illustrated by the impatient question that I have been confronted with on many occasions: *Well, if you don't think the Court should be resolving so many policy matters, how do you think it should handle all those cases that are put in front of it?* In both these instances, what is being presented is a complete inability to imagine that the Constitution does not authoritatively resolve a wide range of public questions, including abortion and innumerable other difficult issues, and that the Court could simply say so.

Of course, if the Court were to overrule *Roe* on the ground that the Constitution provides no resources for deciding when the mother's interest in terminating a pregnancy is more important than the state's interest in protecting the life of the fetus, other cases would be brought. But that does not mean that the courts would have to use the Constitution to resolve those cases. With respect to abortion or, indeed, with respect to most public issues, it is possible for the justices to say again—and again and again—that the Constitution does not provide an authoritative answer to this dispute. The fact is that most of the legal profession cannot conceive of this possibility or, if confronted with it, considers the suggestion heretical. This state of affairs is partly the result of familiarity bred by what I have called the routinization of judicial power and partly the result of the fetishism that has grown up around the idea of a case.

Conclusion

At any rate, we are nearing the end of this book and it is time to take stock. In previous chapters I have tried to convince you that in the modern era we have become accustomed to excessive use of judicial power. The modern pattern has degraded our political discourse, intensified social conflict, drained moral confidence, institutionalized political revenge, undermined local political life, and impoverished the scope and significance of public decision making.

Moreover, I have tried to explain why the way that modern lawyers think about law in general and constitutional interpretation in particular provides no significant brakes on the courts and, indeed, encourages the excessive use of judicial power. Realism, I have said, interacts with legalism in ways that expand the judiciary's imperial role. Devotion to high principle is, in effect, devotion to a kind of moralistic idealism that drives judges to pursue their visions of social progress heedlessly despite their intellectual commitment to self-restraint. Constant evocation of the authority of text, tradition, history, and structure is reassuring but cannot constrain judges because nothing constrains choice as to which authority is decisive in a particular case. Worse, the Supreme Court has treated certain of its precedents as decisive over all other sources of legal authority when its own pre-eminent position is threatened (or thought to be threatened). Thus, if there is a bedrock constraint on the justices' freedom, it is only the felt need to preserve judicial authority. And, when judges choose to rely on the authority of prevailing constitutional doctrines, those doctrines usually direct them to the kinds of political judgments that cannot be made independently of personal identity and philosophy. And, in this final chapter, I have said that the instincts ingrained by legal education and the practice of law also work to encourage the reckless use of power.

It must be quickly added that, as I have said before, the modern use of judicial power has to its credit some valuable accomplishments. Indeed, the Court holds out the constant, ever receding promise of more rescues, reforms and social transformations. The promise is copious enough to include (for some) gay rights, educational equality, and unrestricted self-expression while (for others) it encompasses secure private property, decentralized government, and the right to bear arms. Potentially there is something for virtually every segment of the political spectrum. Except for moments of outrage, whether prompted by the announcement of a right to abortion or by the Court's intervention in a close presidential election, the promise keeps Americans from facing up to the more diffuse damage that the Supreme Court (along with the rest of the judiciary) is doing to our politics and culture.

Of course, I may be wrong to think that these diffuse harms will be deeper and more lasting than the gains from specific reforms. Judgment is made more difficult by the undeniable fact that the concrete gains achieved through judicial decision making can produce diffuse benefits as well as diffuse harms. I am confident, for example, that the Court's equal protection jurisprudence has helped to give various minority groups a sense of hope and self-respect. Free speech decisions have no doubt added to Americans' innate assertiveness and probably have encouraged an ethic of tolerance. Maybe, as some of the justices have suggested, the abortion decisions have helped to induce a sea-change in the way women understand their role in society.

It is equally possible that these benefits, in turn, inflict cultural damage. For instance, minority groups who find self-respect in judicial decisions consequently divert resources from political activity to litigation. And free expression, with excesses constantly protected by the courts, is increasingly coarse and mindless. Maybe in liberating women the right to abortion also undermined stable family structures and, as some fear, even respect for life itself. As with any of the overarching judgments about the shape of a desirable future, the judiciary's proper role cannot be discovered through precise calculation. Too much is incommensurate or beyond measurement or unpredictable. But it can be said, I think, that a sound assessment cannot be made without attention to the kinds of social costs that I have tried to illustrate in this book.

The attention of politicians, scholars, and interested citizens should move from repetitive and largely fruitless debates about the legal justifiability of the various policies mandated by the Court toward a difficult but essential examination of the broader impact of the courts' modern role. Such an examination, I believe, would generate abundant evidence that it is desirable, perhaps imperative, to turn judges and justices from their present course. It is a course that is relatively new in American history, and it is a course that cedes far too much power to the members of a single profession.

In any event, for many decades the subject of judicial lawlessness—in the form of senatorial questions about judicial power to amend the Constitution, to legislate, or to transform society on the basis of personal beliefs—has repeatedly surfaced in confirmation hearings. This, along with the episodic political fury aroused by judicial decisions and the prolonged and almost desperate intellectual effort in the legal academy to find some justification for the Court's modern role, suggests that beneath American reverence for courts and law there is uneasiness about the judiciary's place in our political system.

It is possible that this uneasiness is now or could become strong enough to amount to a judgment that the judiciary's role in modern American politics should be significantly reined in. If so, of course, there would have to be continued attention to the kinds of people who ascend to the bench, although consideration would have to be given to factors that go beyond professional qualifications, likely votes on specific issues, and even judicial philosophy. But, given modern understandings of the nature of law and given the realities of legal education and practice, such an effort would have to go beyond the confirmation process itself to emphasize direct pressure on the judicial system exerted by institutions that are not dominated by the legal profession.

Appendix

Cases Cited

Regents of the Univ. of Cal. v. Bakke, 438 U.S. 265, 269 (opinion of
    Powell, J., announcing the judgment of the Court) (1978).
Brandenburg v. Ohio, 395 U.S. 444 (1969).
Bartnicki v. Vopper, 532 U.S. 514 (2001).
Brown v. Board of Education of Topeka, 347 U.S. 843 (1954).
Bush v. Gore, 531 U.S. 98 (2000).
Cohen v. California, 403 U.S. 15 (1971).
Dred Scott v. Sandford, 60 U.S. 393 (1857).
Ex parte Milligan, 4 Wall. 2 (1865).
Frontiero v. Richardson, 411 U.S. 677, 678
    (Brennan, J. announcing the judgment of the Court) (1973).
Gitlow v. New York, 268 U.S. 652 (1925).
Griswold v. Connecticut, 381 U.S. 479 (1965).
Grutter v. Bollinger, 539 U.S. 306 (2003).
Lawrence v. Texas, 539 U.S. 558 (2003).
Lochner v. New York, 198 U.S. 45 (1905).
Marbury v. Madison, 5 U.S. 137 (1803).
Miranda v. Arizona, 384 U.S. 436 (1966).
New York Times v. Sullivan, 376 U.S. 254 (1964).
New York Times Co. v. United States (Pentagon Papers), 403 U.S. 713
    (1971).
Planned Parenthood of Southeastern Pennsylvania v. Casey, 505 U.S.
    833 (1992).
Plessy v. Ferguson, 163 U.S. 537 (1896).
Roe v. Wade, 410 U.S. 113 (1973).
Roper v. Simmons, 543 U.S. 551 (2005).
Tinker v. Des Moines Independent School District, 393 U.S. 503
    (969).

United States v. Caroline Products Co., 304 U.S. 144 (1938).
United States v. Nixon, 418 U.S. 683 (1974).
Whitney v. California, 274 U.S. 359, 372 (Brandeis, J., concurring)
  (1927).

References

Chapter 1

Blasi, Vincent (ed.). *The Burger Court: The Counter-Revolution that Wasn't*. New Haven, 1984.

Casper, Jonathan D. "The Supreme Court and National Policy Making." *American Political Science Review* 70 (1976).

Comiskey, Michael. *Seeking Justices: The Judging of Supreme Court Nominees*. Lawrence, KS, 2004.

Dahl, Robert A. "Decision-making in a Democracy: The Supreme Court as a National Policy-Maker." *Journal of Public Law* 6 (1957).

Dworkin, Ronald. "From Bork to Kennedy." *New York Review of Books* XXXIV (1987).

Dworkin, Ronald. *Law's Empire*. Cambridge, MA, 1986.

Dworkin, Ronald, *Taking Rights Seriously*. Cambridge, MA, 1977.

Ely, John Hart. "The Wages of Crying Wolf: A Comment on *Roe v. Wade*." *Yale Law Journal* 82 (1973).

Farrelly, David G. "The Senate Judiciary Committee: Qualifications of Members." *American Political Science Review* 37 (1943).

Friedman, Barry. "The Birth of an Academic Obsession: The History of the Countermajoritarian Difficulty, Part Five." *Yale Law Journal* 112 (2002).

Keck, Thomas E. *The Most Activist Supreme Court in History: The Road to Modern Judicial Conservatism*. Chicago, 2004.

Kramer, Larry D. "Forward: We the Court." *Harvard Law Review* 115 (2001).

Miller, Mark C. *The High Priests of American Politics: The Role of Lawyers in American Political Institutions*. Knoxville, 1995.

Perry, H.W., Jr., Powe, L.A., Jr. "The Political Battle for the Constitution." *Constitutional Commentary* 21 (2006).

Posner, Richard A. *Breaking the Deadlock: The 2000 Election, the Constitution, and the Courts*. Princeton, 2001.

U.S. Senate Committee on the Judiciary. *Nomination of Warren Burger to Be an Associate Justice of the United States Supreme Court: Hearings Before the Senate Judiciary Committee*. 91 Cong., 1st sess., 1969.

U.S. Senate Committee on the Judiciary. Nomination of Robert H. Bork to Be Associate Justice of the Supreme Court of the United States: Hearings before the Senate Judiciary Committee, 100th Cong., 1st sess., 1987.

Chapter 2

Bickel, Alexander. *The Least Dangerous Branch: The Supreme Court at the Bar of Politics*. Indianapolis, 1962.

Bollinger, Lee C., *The Tolerant Society: Freedom of Speech and Extremist Speech in America*. New York, 1986.

Burt, Robert A. "Constitutional Law and the Teaching of the Parables." *Yale Law Journal* 93 (1984).

Chayes, Abram. "The Role of the Judge in Public Law Litigation." *Harvard Law Review* 89 (1976), 1281-1316.

Clinton, Robert Lowry. *Marbury v. Madison and Judicial Review*. Lawrence, KS, 1989.

Comiskey, Michael. *Seeking Justices: The Judging of Supreme Court Nominees*. Lawrence, KS, 2004.

Dahl, Robert. "Decision-Making in a Democracy: The Supreme Court as National Policy-Maker." *Journal of Public Law* 6 (1957), 279-295.

Dinan, John J. *Keeping the People's Liberties: Legislators, Citizens, and Judges as Guardians of Rights*. Lawrence, KS, 1998.

Eisenberg, Theodore, Yeazell, Stephen C. "The Ordinary and the Extraordinary in Institutional Litigation," *Harvard Law Review* 93 (1980), 465-517.

Ely, John Hart. *Democracy and Distrust: A Theory of Judicial Review*. Cambridge, MA, 1980.

Frankfurter, Felix, Greene, Nathan, *The Labor Injunction,* New York, 1930.

Fiss, Owen. "Foreward: The Forms of Justice." *Harvard Law Review* 93 (1979).

Kramer, Larry D. *The People Themselves: Popular Constitutionalism and Judicial Review*. New York, 2004.

Linde, Hans. "Are State Constitutions Common Law?" *Arizona Law Review* 34 (1992), 215-229.

Nelson, William E. *Marbury v. Madison: The Origins and Legacy of Judicial Review*. Lawrence, KS, 2000.

Rakove, Jack N. *Original Meanings: Politics and Ideas in the Making of the Constitution*. New York, 1996.

Redish, Martin H. "Judicial Review and the 'Political Question.'" *Northwestern University Law Review* 79 (1984/85), 1031-1061.

Rehnquist, William H. *All the Laws But One: Civil Liberties in Wartime*. New York, 1998.

Rosenberg, Gerald N. *The Hollow Hope: Can Courts Bring About Social Change?* Chicago, London, 1991.

Stevens, Robert Bocking. *Law School: Legal Education in America from the 1850s to the 1980s*. Chapel Hill, London, 1983.

Thayer, James B. "The Origin and Scope of the American Doctrine of Constitutional Law." *Harvard Law Review* 7 (1893), 129-156.

Surrency Erwin C. *History of the Federal Courts*. Dobbs Ferry, New York, 2002.

Van Alstyne, William W. "A Critical Guide to *Marbury v. Madison*." *Duke Law Journal* 1969 (1969), 1-47.

Wolfe, Christopher. *The Rise of Modern Judicial Review: From Constitutional Interpretation to Judge-Made Law*. New York, 1986.

Chapter 3

Alexander, Larry, Frederick Schauer. "On Extrajudicial Constitutional Interpretation." *Harvard Law Review* 110 (1977).

Chermerinsky, Erwin. "Foreward: The Vanishing Constitution." *Harvard Law Review* 103 (1989).

Frank, Robert H., Cook, Philip J. *The Winner Take-All Society: Why the Few at the Top Get So Much More than the Rest of Us*. New York, 1995.

Keck, Thomas M. *The Most Activist Supreme Court in History: The Road to Modern Judicial Conservatism*. Chicago, 2004.

Klarman, Michael J. *From Jim Crow to Civil Rights: The Supreme Court and the Struggle for Racial Equality.* New York, 2004.

Nagel, Robert F. *Constitutional Cultures: The Mentality and Consequences of Judicial Review.* Berkeley, 1989.

Nagel, Robert F. *The Implosion of American Federalism.* Oxford, 2001.

Rosenberg, Gerald N. *The Hollow Hope: Can Courts Bring About Social Change?* Chicago, 1991.

Chapter 4

Black, Charles L., Jr. *The Occasions of Justice: Essays Mostly on Law*, 89-102, New York, 1963.

U.S. Senate Committee on the Judiciary. *Nomination of William J. Brennan to Be an Associate Justice of the United States Supreme Court: Hearings Before the Senate Judiciary Committee.* 85 Cong., 1st sess., 1957.

U.S. Senate Committee on the Judiciary. *Nomination of Warren Burger to Be an Associate Justice of the United States Supreme Court: Hearings Before the Senate Judiciary Committee.* 91 Cong., 1st sess., 1969.

U.S. Senate Committee on the Judiciary. *Nomination of Harry Blackmun to Be an Associate Justice of the United States Supreme Court: Hearings Before the Senate Judiciary Committee.* 91 Cong., 2nd sess., 1970.

U.S. Senate Committee on the Judiciary. *Nomination of Lewis Powell to Be an Associate Justice of the United States Supreme Court: Hearings Before the Senate Judiciary Committee.* 92 Cong., 1st sess., 1971.

U.S. Senate Committee on the Judiciary. *Nomination of William Rehnquist to Be an Associate Justice of the United States Supreme Court: Hearings Before the Senate Judiciary Committee.* 92 Cong., 1st sess., 1971.

U.S. Senate Committee on the Judiciary. *Nomination of John Paul Stevens to Be an Associate Justice of the United States Supreme Court: Hearings Before the Senate Judiciary Committee.* 94 Cong., 1st sess., 1975.

U.S. Senate Committee on the Judiciary. *Nomination of Sandra Day O'Connor to Be an Associate Justice of the United States Supreme Court: Hearings Before the Senate Judiciary Committee.* 97 Cong., 1st sess., 1981.

U.S. Senate Committee on the Judiciary. *Nomination of Antonin Scalia to Be an Associate Justice of the United States Supreme Court: Hearings Before the Senate Judiciary Committee.* 99 Cong., 2nd sess., 1986.

U.S. Senate Committee on the Judiciary. *Nomination of Anthony M. Kennedy to Be an Associate Justice of the United States Supreme Court: Hearings Before the Senate Judiciary Committee.* 100 Cong., 1st sess., 1987.

U.S. Senate Committee on the Judiciary. *Nomination of David Souter to Be an Associate Justice of the United States Supreme Court: Hearings Before the Senate Judiciary Committee.* 101 Cong., 2nd sess., 1990.

U.S. Senate Committee on the Judiciary. *Nomination of Clarence Thomas to Be an Associate Justice of the United States Supreme Court: Hearings Before the Senate Judiciary Committee.* 102d Cong., 1st sess., 1991.

U.S. Senate Committee on the Judiciary. *Nomination of Ruth Bader Ginsburg to Be an Associate Justice of the United States Supreme Court: Hearings Before the Senate Judiciary Committee.* 103 Cong., 1st sess., 1993.

U.S. Senate Committee on the Judiciary. *Nomination of Steven G. Breyer to Be an Associate Justice of the United States Supreme Court: Hearings Before the Senate Judiciary Committee.* 103 Cong., 2nd sess., 1994.

U.S. Senate Committee on the Judiciary. *Nomination of John Roberts to Be Chief Justice of the United States Supreme Court: Hearings Before the Senate Judiciary Committee.* 109 Cong., 1st sess., 2005.

U.S. Senate Committee on the Judiciary. *Nomination of Samuel Alito to Be an Associate Justice of the United States Supreme Court: Hearings Before the Senate Judiciary Committee.* 109 Cong., 2nd sess., 2005.

Wechsler, Herbert. "Toward Neutral Principles of Constitutional Law." *Harvard Law Review* 73 (1959).

Chapter 5

Clinton, Robert Lowry. *Marbury v. Madison and Judicial Review.* Lawrence, KS, 1989.

Kramer, Larry D. " Foreward: We the Court." *Harvard Law Review* 115 (2001).

Nelson, William E. *Marbury v. Madison: The Origins and Legacy of Judicial Review.* Lawrence, KS, 2000.

Redish, Martin H. "Judicial Review and the 'Political Question." *Northwestern University Law Review* 79 (1985).

Smith, Steven D. *Law's Quandary.* Cambridge, MA, 2004.

Stoner, James R., Jr. *Common-Law Liberty: Rethinking American Constitutionalism.* Lawrence, Ks. 2003.

Van Alstyne, William W. "A Critical Guide to *Marbury v. Madison.*" *Duke Law Journal* 1969 (1969).

Wolfe, Christopher. *The Rise of Modern Judicial Review: From Constitutional Interpretation to Judge-Made Law.* New York, 1986.

Chapter 6

Bickel, Alexander. *The Least Dangerous Branch: The Supreme Court at the Bar of Politics.* Indianapolis, 1962.

Bickel, Alexander. *The Supreme Court and the Idea of Progress.* New Haven, 1970.

Bickel, Alexander *The Morality of Consent.* New Haven, 1975.

Gunther, Gerald. "The Subtle Vices of the 'Passive Virtues'—A Comment on Principle and Expediency in Judicial Review." *Columbia Law Review* 64 (1964).

Kronman, Anthony T. "Alexander Bickel's Philosophy of Prudence." *Yale Law Journal* 94 (1985).

Wechsler, Herbert. "Reviews." *Yale Law Journal* 75 (1966).

Chapter 7

Barnett, Randy E. "Scalia's Infidelity: A Critique of 'Faint-Hearted' Originalism." *University of Cincinnati Law Review* 75 (2006).

Brest, Paul. "The Misconceived Quest for the Original Understanding." *Boston University Law Review.* 60, 1980).

U.S. Senate Committee on the Judiciary. *Nomination of Antonin Scalia to Be an Associate Justice of the United States Supreme Court: Hearings Before the Senate Judiciary Committee.* 99 Cong., 2nd sess., 1986.

U.S. Senate Committee on the Judiciary. *Nomination of Samuel Alito to Be an Associate Justice of the United States Supreme Court: Hearings Before the Senate Judiciary Committee.* 109 Cong., 2nd sess., 2005.

Chapter 8

Carrington, Paul D. "Diversity!" *Utah Law Review* 1992 (1992).
Dworkin, Ronald. "Lord Devlin and the Enforcement of Morals." *Yale Law Journal* 75 (1996).
Lawrence, Charles R III. "Each Other's Harvest: Diversity's Deeper Meaning." *University of San Francisco Law Review* 31 (1997).
Levinson, Sanford. *Wrestling with Diversity*. Durham, 2003.
Mill, John Stuart. *On Liberty*. Haldeman-Julius Co. 1925 (originally published 1859).
Post, Robert. "Introduction." In Post, Robert, Rogin, Michael, eds., *Race and Representation: Affirmative Action*. New York, 1988.
Powell, H. Jefferson. *A Community Built on Words: The Constitution in History and Politics*. Chicago, 2002.
Schuck, Peter H. *Diversity in America: Keeping Government at a Safe Distance*. Cambridge, MA, 2003.
Sullivan, Kathleen M. "Comment, Sins of Discrimination: Last Term's Affirmative Action Cases." *Harvard Law Review* 78 (1986).
Waldron, Jeremy. *Law and Disagreement*. Oxford, 1999.
White, James Boyd. "What's Wrong with Our Talk about Race? On History, Particularity, and Affirmative Action." *Michigan Law Review* 100 (2002).
Wood, Peter. *Diversity: The Invention of a Concept*. San Francisco, 2003.

Chapter 9

Althouse Ann. "No Exit." *Wall Street Journal*. A9 (October 21, 2006).
Bolick, Clint. *David's Hammer: The Case for an Activist Judiciary*. Washington, D.C., 2007.
Daicoff, Susan. "Lawyer, Know Thyself: A Review of Empirical Research on Attorney Attributes Bearing on Professionalism." *American University Law Review* 46 (1997).
Daicoff, Susan Swaim. *Lawyer, Know Thyself: A Psychological Analysis of Personality Strengths and Weaknesses*. Washington, D.C., 2004.
Dworkin, Ronald. *Taking Rights Seriously*. Cambridge, MA, 1977.
Klarman, Michael. "*Bush v. Gore* through the Lens of Constitutional History." *University of California Law Review* 89 (2001).
Llewellyn, Karl. *The Case Law System in America*. Chicago, 1989.
Miller, Mark C. *The High Priests of American Politics: The Role of Lawyers in American Political Institutions*. Knoxville, 1995.
Posner, Richard. A. *The Problems of Jurisprudence*. Cambridge, MA, 1990.
Rudenstine David. *The Day the Presses Stopped: A History of the Pentagon Papers Case*. Berkeley, 1996.
Sullivan, William M., Colby, Anne, Wegner, Judith Welch, Bond, Lloyd, Shulman, Lee S. *Educating Lawyers: Preparation for the Profession of Law*. San Francisco, 2007
Sunstein Cass. "Order without Law." *University of Chicago Law Review* 68 (2001).
Wice, Paul, *Judges & Lawyers: The Human Side of Justice*. New York, 1991.

Index